OUTDOOR CHURCH

Text copyright © Sally Welch 2016
The author asserts the moral right to be identified as the author of this work

Published by
The Bible Reading Fellowship
15 The Chambers, Vineyard
Abingdon OX14 3FE
United Kingdom
Tel: +44 (0)1865 319700
Email: enquiries@brf.org.uk
Website: www.brf.org.uk
BRF is a Registered Charity

ISBN 978 0 85746 416 3

First published 2016
10 9 8 7 6 5 4 3 2 1 0

Acknowledgements
Unless otherwise stated, scripture quotations are from The New Revised Standard
Version of the Bible, Anglicised edition, copyright © 1989, 1995 by the Division of
Christian Education of the National Council of the Churches of Christ in the United
States of America. Used by permission. All rights reserved.

Scripture quotations taken from The Holy Bible, New International Version (Anglicised
edition) copyright © 1979, 1984, 2011 by Biblica. Used by permission of Hodder
& Stoughton Publishers, an Hachette UK company. All rights reserved.'NIV' is a
registered trademark of Biblica. UK trademark number 1448790.

Scripture quotations taken from the Holy Bible, English Standard Version, published by
HarperCollins Publishers, © 2001 Crossway Bibles, a division of Good News Publishers.
Used by permission. All rights reserved.

Extracts from *The Barnabas Children's Bible* by Rhona Davies (Barnabas for Children,
2012) are copyright © 2007 Anno Domini Publishing. Used by kind permission.

Cover and inside illustrations © Sarah Dunning

Every effort has been made to trace and contact copyright owners for material used
in this resource. We apologise for any inadvertent omissions or errors, and would ask
those concerned to contact us so that full acknowledgement can be made in the future.

A catalogue record for this book is available from the British Library

Printed and bound by CPI Group (UK) Ltd, Croydon CR0 4YY

SALLY WELCH

OUTDOOR CHURCH

20 sessions to take church outside
the building for children and families

Important Information

Photocopying permission

The right to photocopy material in *Outdoor Church* is granted for the pages that contain the photocopying clause: 'Reproduced with permission from *Outdoor Church* by Sally Welch, published by Barnabas for Children, 2016', so long as reproduction is for use in a teaching situation by the original purchaser. The right to photocopy material is not granted for anyone other than the original purchaser without written permission from BRF.

The Copyright Licensing Agency (CLA)

If you are resident in the UK and you have a photocopying licence with the Copyright Licensing Agency (CLA) please check the terms of your licence. If your photocopying request falls within the terms of your licence, you may proceed without seeking further permission. If your request exceeds the terms of your CLA licence, please contact the CLA directly with your request. Copyright Licensing Agency, Saffron House, 6–10 Kirby Street, London EC1N 8TS. Telephone 020 7400 3100; fax 020 7400 3101; email cla@cla.co.uk; website www.cla.co.uk. The CLA will provide photocopying authorisation and royalty fee information on behalf of BRF.

BRF is a Registered Charity (No. 233280)

Contents

Parables and festivals:

Spring

Summer

Autumn

Winter

Introduction

In 2012 the National Trust published a report entitled *Natural Childhood*, which highlighted the growing alienation of children from outdoor spaces and the contact with nature that these spaces provide. The report used the term 'nature deficit disorder', first coined in 2005 by Richard Louv to describe this alienation. Although not a medical condition, nature deficit disorder none the less carries with it a great cost to human well-being, most notably in the loss of a sense of connectedness and relationship with the rest of the world, and difficulty in acknowledging one's own place within it. Much publicity surrounded the report and many initiatives have developed from it, linking with those organisations and groups that were already trying to address the disconnection between human beings and the natural world.

Within a Christian context, the steady growth of interest in Celtic spirituality has demonstrated a growing enthusiasm for developing a relationship with God in and through nature. The Forest Church movement has taken this one step further, having at its heart a vision drawn from ancient Christian practice when many sacred places were outside, but also recognising contemporary research into the benefits of time spent out of doors. Forest Church emphasises that it isn't just 'church outside' but that it aims to participate with creation; Outdoor Church has a similar vision but acknowledges that time, environment and other restrictions can mean that a different approach may be necessary.

Outdoor Church explores the relationship of groups and individuals with each other and with the natural world in ways that are most appropriate for them. It offers freedom and space to discover aspects of God revealed in and through his creation. There is scope to evolve and develop a style and pace of worship and relationship that is appropriate to the community and the individuals within it, while holding to the aims of spending time in the natural world, being at one with creation and participating in the endless cycle of praise to the creator. Outdoor Church can be a regular way of worship for a community or group, or simply a one-off or occasional event that stimulates an appreciation of the local landscape and environment. It can be for a group of adults and children or used simply for children's activity days or holiday clubs. The essence of Outdoor Church is freedom, both in its relationship with nature and in the way Outdoor Church resources are used.

USING THIS BOOK

This book is organised in two parts, with the first containing some arguments in favour of Outdoor Church events, as well as information and advice on their preparation and delivery. The second part offers seasonal activities and crafts based on the parables of Jesus, which themselves drew on the natural world to invite listeners to a deeper understanding of the kingdom of God. The activities are structured as events, with a regular programme which can be followed completely or divided into separate resources according to the requirements of the worshipping group.

At the end of each season are some suggestions for celebrating a related festival, which, again, can be used as individual components incorporated into regular worship or as a complete event in themselves. Some suggestions for prayers are also included, but it is understood that an Outdoor Church event is in itself an act of worship, with each discovery a prayer in itself: 'God writes the Gospel not in the Bible alone, but on trees and flowers and clouds and stars' (attributed to Martin Luther).

WHAT IS OUTDOOR CHURCH, AND WHY SHOULD WE HOLD AN OUTDOOR CHURCH EVENT?

The first book of the Bible, Genesis, contains the well-known story of creation. God's loving action is demonstrated not only in the imaginative care that is poured into his new world, but in the fact that, after making it, he blesses it—and this blessing is not restricted to humankind but applies to all God's works. However, evidence that God's love extends throughout his creation, and can be seen shining in and through that creation, is found throughout the entire Bible. The whole book rejoices in the capacity of nature to reveal not only God's love for the world and those who inhabit it, but also his power, his wisdom, his might, his endless creativity and imagination, and his tender care for every detail. 'It is he who made the earth by his power, who established the world by his wisdom, and by his understanding stretched out the heavens,' writes Jeremiah (Jeremiah 51:15). Even when Job is locked in his most bitter dispute with God about the unfairness of his life, he acknowledges God's universal power:

But ask the animals, and they will teach you; the birds of the air, and they will tell you; ask the plants of the earth, and they will teach you; and the fish of the sea will declare to you. Who among all these does not know that the hand of the Lord has done this? In his hand is the life of every living thing and the breath of every human being. (Job 12:7–10)

This world has been damaged and distorted by sin, but glimpses of God's glory can still be perceived not only through nature but within it. With these glimpses comes the promise of a future time of restoration. The book of Isaiah asserts God's love for his creation constantly and shares the vision of a redeemed world with the arrival of the Messiah, when warring factions and discord will cease: 'The wolf shall live with the lamb, the leopard shall lie down with the kid, the calf and the lion and the fatling together, and a little child shall lead them' (Isaiah 11:6).

With the birth of Christ, the potential for the redemption of the created world and its restoration is realised. Christ the creator enters the world he created: 'All things came into being through him, and without him not one thing came into being' (John 1:3). Jesus enters this world to redeem it with and through his love: 'For God so loved the world…' (John 3:16). He becomes part of the creation and meets God through it. The wilderness becomes a place of testing and of prayer; hills and mountains become sites where he can find the peace he needs to wrestle with his will; even storms are part of his experience, demonstrating his willingness to become involved with all aspects of the natural world.

Nor was this involvement with and in creation limited to his own personal spirituality. In his parables, Christ constantly uses examples taken from nature to illustrate aspects of God's kingdom and of our own behaviour within it. We are taught to appreciate the vast expanses of fields and landscapes, but also to learn from the details of flowers and the behaviour of birds. In this we do no more than reflect that characteristic of God which cherishes every single aspect of his creation.

This teaching continues throughout the New Testament, with the writers of the letters celebrating God's action in the world and the value of his creation: 'Ever since the creation of the world his eternal power and divine nature, invisible though they are, have been understood and seen through the things he has made' (Romans 1:20). The role of Christ within the world, both in creation and the redemption of that creation after the actions of humankind corrupted and inverted the order of things, is constantly emphasised: Jesus is 'the image of the invisible God, the firstborn of all creation. For by him all things were created, in heaven and on earth, visible and invisible, whether thrones or dominions or rulers or authorities—all things were created through him and for him' (Colossians 1:15–16, ESV). Finally, in Revelation, we are given a glimpse of the new order, when heaven and earth are recreated and restoration is complete: 'Then I saw a new heaven and a new earth; for the first heaven and the first earth had passed away, and the sea was no more' (Revelation 21:1).

It is important to recognise that human beings are not set above this order, but are part of it. In Genesis 1:28, men and women are given stewardship over the rest of the created world. We are expected to work with it and for it, putting it to good use and adapting it as we work, but we are told that we must accomplish this in a way that is responsible and mindful not just of human beings but of the whole of creation, endeavouring to ensure the flourishing of the entire natural world. Our 'dominion' over nature should be that of a watchful, caring influence, encouraging cooperation and mutual sustainability. This attitude reaches its fulfilment for Christians in the Eucharist: grapes and wheat that have been planted, tended and harvested by human beings, working in harmony with nature, are made into bread and wine and offered back to God in memory of Christ's redemptive and restorative action on the cross. The Eucharist looks back to the first creation and forward to the re-creation in Revelation, which are linked outside time and space by Christ's love, joining us in community to each other and to God.

A willingness to learn from and rejoice in the gifts of the natural world is part of our Christian heritage, which continues beyond the Bible into the Christian tradition. The integrated life of work and prayer put forth by St Benedict in his Rule is a holistic way of living that encourages us to become fully engaged in our daily existence and to follow Christ in all that we do. The spirituality of St Francis, with his close and intense relationship with nature and his deep passion for God's power and love manifested in creation, broke through the medieval habit of thinking about nature as merely utilitarian, and demonstrated another way of living in harmony with all that God had made.

Celtic spirituality, too, celebrates the presence of God in the wilder places, with evidence of his wisdom, power and love being found in those parts of the world that are more remote. These landscapes reflect the simplicity and harmony with God's will that are goals of human spirituality. Through his existence on earth, Christ made the world holy; the continuing presence of the Holy Spirit sustains and supports us as we meet with God in and through the natural world.

However, despite the excellence of these examples and the general recognition of the importance of the natural world to the well-being of those who inhabit it, there is today an increasingly large disconnection between people and nature, and this is nowhere more acutely witnessed than in the behaviour and experience of children. According to the Royal Society for the Protection of Birds (RSPB), only one child in five feels connected to nature, and only one in ten regularly plays in wild spaces. The amount of time spent overall in playing outside has halved in a generation, and research has demonstrated that those who do not spend time outdoors as children are less motivated in their concern for the environment as adults. These adults in their turn spend less time engaged in outdoor pursuits, and their attitude is handed on to the next generation of children, so that we are in danger of creating a population that knows little and cares less about the impact of their lives and lifestyles on the environment. Worse still, they will lack the opportunity and inclination to discover for themselves the joy and wonder of exploring the natural world and the way in which it can illustrate the loving purposes of God.

The findings of the 2012 *Natural Childhood* inquiry, sponsored by the National Trust, cited barriers such as the increasing amount of indoor entertainment available, the amount of dangerous, fast-moving traffic, and the lack of green space. Combined with a culture that is perhaps overly concerned with health and safety, these factors produce (as mentioned in the Introduction to this book) a generation of children who are suffering from what Richard Louv called 'nature deficit disorder'—a state of alienation from nature. Adults and children alike need natural space in order to understand their relationship with the world and its people; Christians need the opportunity to see the love of God for his creation, which is so great that not a single sparrow can fall without his knowledge (Matthew 10:29), and the most ordinary flower is clothed with extraordinary beauty, detailed down to its smallest petal (6:29). By observing creation, we can find an understanding of the creator. Even those parts of nature that we find ugly and unappealing serve to give a fuller and rounder appreciation of our multifaceted God.

Yet we must not simply use nature as a way of illustrating God's characteristics. We must not simply admire nature because God made it—for his creation is more than that. Every microscopic seed, perfect in tiny detail, every mountain peak and vast ocean, all are resplendent with the entire personality of God. Each particle is given its being through and with God, and, by understanding this, we can begin to appreciate some of the depth and character and imagination and love of the God who made it all.

In learning to love and understand nature, we gain an understanding not only of God but of ourselves. Acts of indifference towards nature or a disregard for our surroundings and the creatures with which we share them lead us to devalue ourselves and our place within the sphere of God's world. Outdoor Church celebrates the wholeness, the interdependence and the interconnectedness of all created things, while being mindful that 'truth, beauty and goodness is only intimated in nature but disclosed in Christ. It will not be found in nature, only in Christ' (Alister McGrath, *The Open Secret*, Blackwell, 2008). By spending time in open spaces, however small or insignificant they seem, we can learn more about God and each other through our interaction with the outdoors. Outdoor worship, activities and community events can all contribute to a greater understanding of nature and, in and through nature, of God. 'Before the mountains were brought forth, or ever you had formed the earth and the world, from everlasting to everlasting you are God' (Psalm 90:2).

Getting started with Outdoor Church

Choosing your venue

Perhaps the greatest challenge that faces anyone beginning to consider Outdoor Church is that of selecting an appropriate venue for the event or series of events. There are some fortunate churches in rural locations that are situated in the middle of a sizeable area of land with plenty of different types of landscape, clear boundaries and easy access points. These, however, are the lucky few; most of the rest of us will have limited access to a limited type of environment, with some groups struggling to find anywhere to meet outside that is even slightly conducive to worship, reflection and craft activities. In these cases, creative and imaginative use of the environments that we can access becomes vitally important.

The ideal location for an Outdoor Church event is a large wooded area with a variety of trees, flowers and bushes, with access to a small pond that is fed by a stream, possibly bordered with large rocks and stones; or an area of trees near the seashore, with cliffs and rockpools. The location should contain a storage facility, an area for food-related activities and a fire pit, and should be easily accessible by road, yet remote enough for the sounds of the manufactured environment not to intrude. It is tempting, when faced with a list of requirements as extensive as this, to give up completely, but it is possible to create an Outdoor Church site from very limited space and resources.

The first step in selecting a site is to consider those aspects of Outdoor Church that are most important for your group. If it is essential that the venue should be quiet and far from traffic noise, this may mean that access will be more difficult. Equally, if fire-lighting and edible crafts are attractive, a venue with a water supply may take priority over one with a more wooded landscape. Do remember to ask permission if you wish to light a fire on property that is not your own. Fires carry serious risks, particularly during the dry summer season, and must always be dealt with responsibly. Most public environments do not permit open fires, although some national forests provide barbecue places.

Perhaps the best thing to do first is to make a list of your requirements and the order of their importance to you and your group. This is an activity best undertaken by the group itself, including any children, so that all can be involved in the selection of the site from the very beginning.

The next step is to familiarise yourself with the area in which you wish Outdoor Church to take place. Walk around the area, taking note of each open space, the facilities it could offer and any indication as to who owns it. This too can be undertaken by the group, working in small teams to cover the maximum amount of ground as quickly as possible.

Once a list of potential locations has been compiled, select the five best sites and investigate how they might be accessed. Don't discount areas of land that are in private ownership; many landowners are very aware of the tenuous relationship that both adults and children have with the natural environment and are keen to support educational initiatives that address it.

Remember that your Outdoor Church can take place in several different venues or just one. Your group might feel that a focused relationship with one site through the different seasons might be beneficial, or they might prefer to gain experience of different types of landscapes. Compare your list of worship requirements against the offerings of land and see which options are the closest match. Do not forget, however, that safety should be the top priority for all venues: for example, if the environment is an open one, how will boundaries be marked? If the group will be in view of the general public, how will this affect the atmosphere or the worship? Is the event going to be a closed one or will it have permeable boundaries and times (a more challenging option)? If access is complicated, how can emergency vehicles reach the site, and what arrangements can be made for people with disabilities?

If the group, or the group leader, feels that a major Outdoor Church initiative will be too challenging at first, a smaller, more domestic space might be preferable. Look for a corner of a local recreation ground or a small park instead, or investigate to see if any local houses have large gardens or areas within their land that are not lawns or flowerbeds. Do not overlook the potential of a churchyard, particularly one that is closed for burials. Wildlife areas within churchyards can answer many needs and have the additional advantage of being easily controlled with regard to access.

If even an area of churchyard is unobtainable, smaller areas can still provide an outside space. A concrete yard can be provided with pots of flowers and herbs or raised beds, with bird feeders and piles of logs to encourage wildlife, and it will have the advantage of being easy to keep tidy as well. If there is no outside space at all, then move Outdoor Church inside: have an area of your church enclosed, or build some stage-set trees and scenery. Bring in pots of flowers and herbs, ant houses and wormeries, giant snails and other wildlife. Have an aquarium or small water feature: even a child's sand or water tray can be filled with soil and water. Better to begin with what is available, however small or urban it may seem, than never to begin at all.

Safety considerations

Statistics from the Consumer Safety Unit of the Department of Trade and Industry reveal that a domestic accident requiring hospital treatment is more than twice as likely to happen indoors than outside. The 2012 National Trust report *Natural Childhood* highlights taking risks and learning to become independent as key factors in healthy physical, emotional and mental development. The report argues that being exposed to risk enables children to learn about their personal physical and psychological limits. Outdoor activities with an element of danger stimulate children to think and care for themselves and others in a group, and will add a dimension of interest and challenge that is highly beneficial.

All children should be given equal opportunities to experience the outdoors in ways that are unmediated by too much adult intervention. The varieties of challenges that arise when worshipping outside in different weather conditions, some of which may not be entirely pleasant, offer an experience that is comparatively rare in contemporary society but presents a new perspective not only on the natural world but on one's ability to cope with adverse conditions, whether mental or physical. For this reason, Outdoor Church events should take place, as far as possible, in whatever weather conditions present themselves. The normal outdoor experiences of being stung by nettles, scratched by brambles and occasionally bruised by falls or trips should be accepted as part of the event, although first aid should always be on hand.

The attitude of accompanying adults can have a significant influence on the way in which adverse conditions and events are dealt with by children. Cheerful, confident, uncomplaining adults, unconcerned by the effect of rain, cold and so on, who present a sympathetic but not over-protective attitude, will enable children to develop courage and independence, accepting occasional hurts as part of the learning process.

However, an Outdoor Church event should always endeavour to be as safe as possible, and the risks that are experienced should be carefully managed so that all activities can be undertaken safely and in a controlled way. Preventable injury is never acceptable, and efforts to make an Outdoor Church site and those who use it safe should be constant and ongoing. Safety measures should be under regular review and continually updated as seasons and activities change.

One of the most important factors in ensuring a safe Outdoor Church event is to have a clear understanding of roles and responsibilities within the group, particularly among the leaders. It is a good idea to have a designated safety leader, who is not the worship leader but is responsible for ensuring safety precautions on the site and during the journey towards it. Ideally the safety leader should be a qualified First Aider; certainly they should be in possession of a well-equipped first aid kit that includes all the normal medicines, insect bite and sting relief ointments, antibacterial hand gel and sun cream.

Before meeting at a site for the first time, or if the site is used infrequently, the safety leader should inspect the site for possible hazards and for any changes to the environment that may have occurred since the last gathering. If the Outdoor

Church site has specific boundaries, these can be inspected; if the group has artificial boundaries such as marks on trees, or ribbons, these can be put in place. The safety leader should be the first point of contact for any accidents or incidents and, in the event of a crisis, should be the communication point between the gathering and outside agencies. The safety leader should always carry their mobile phone (ensuring it is charged), as well as a list of useful numbers.

However, it is important that the group recognises that the safety of an Outdoor Church event is the responsibility of everyone present. Parents are responsible for their own children but should also be aware of the activities of other children, while the children themselves should be encouraged to act responsibly and sociably, helping their peers if they spot a difficulty and informing adults about potential hazards on-site or in the behaviour of others. These safety measures will be greatly helped if the activities are all-age and group-focused, rather than involving the separation of children from adults or individuals from one another. Times of quiet meditation and the experience of solitude can be managed even in the context of a group if agreement on maintaining silence is reached.

It is a good idea to agree, within the group, on principles of safety for the whole community. For example, one child may be allowed by their parents to climb trees, which, in the context of an Outdoor Church event, may be considered too dangerous. Rules agreed corporately, with children included, are more likely to be adhered to, especially if the reason for their imposition is understood. Fire and water safety rules, in particular, need to be agreed and enforced strictly, for the safety of the whole community. These rules should be available at all times and referred to frequently, so that they become part of the natural lore of the community. An emergency evacuation plan might also be necessary, agreed upon by the group, with regular reminders given as to its contents.

The starting and finishing time for events should be made clear on publicity and at the event itself. It should be decided when corporate responsibility begins and ends—whether this is at the beginning of the event itself, when people arrive at the site, or on the journey to and from the site. Ensure that the group is made aware of what is to happen, where it will happen and when it will finish. It is a good idea to adopt a signal for the beginning and ending of an event—the ringing of a bell, perhaps, or whistle-blowing. This can also have the effect of enabling expectation to build and behaviour to adapt for the beginning of a more focused time of worship and prayer.

The boundaries of the site should be corporately agreed upon and clearly marked so that the group is aware of them and does not move beyond them during some of the more adventurous exercises. If the site has natural boundaries, such as walls or hedges, agreement will be easy to reach. If the site is harder to define, ribbons or flags can be tied at frequent intervals around trees and other landmarks. Balloons, though cheerful, are not so good, due to their propensity to pop! Any artificial boundary markers should be removed by the safety leader at the end of the event.

One of the most effective safety measures when interacting with the natural world is to wear the correct clothing. People who are dry and warm will experience higher levels of enjoyment and appreciation than those who are cold and damp. Encourage those attending the event to dress appropriately: waterproofs should always be taken, with boots or stout shoes an imperative. Protective clothing is just as important during the summer as in winter: long-sleeved tops and sun hats are advisable, as well as frequent application of sun cream. It is a good idea for the safety leader to look up the weather forecast for the event and communicate with those on the attendance contact list, so that good choices about clothing can be made in advance.

In addition to general instructions concerning boundaries and behaviour, the group safety rules should contain specific information regarding food, fire and water safety. As always, the behaviour of the adults will influence that of the children: if it is necessary for child safety that certain rules are kept, the best way to ensure that this happens is for the adults of a group to keep them too, even if it is less necessary for them to do so.

No plants are to be eaten unless a leader says they are OK, and adults should be reminded not to eat anything that they are not 100 per cent sure is safe. Local Nature Conservancy organisations can give specific information on which plants within a particular area are dangerous or poisonous. You might even invite an expert to a gathering to share their knowledge. Hands should be cleaned with antibacterial gel before people eat anything, whether the food is provided by the group or gathered on-site.

Fires are wonderful for community building but present obvious hazards. A fire pit should be dug, ideally with the involvement of the whole group, and a safety line marked out, beyond which those not involved in tending the fire should not go. A fire blanket should be provided, along with water in containers that are not a hazard in themselves (that is, jerry cans with screw tops rather than open buckets of water).

Remember that small children can drown in only a few inches of water, including buckets and washing-up bowls. Puddles, pools and streams should have safety zones, and small children should be carefully watched when interacting with them. Rainfall can change the safety levels of an environment quite rapidly, swelling streams and filling ditches with water.

Any tools should be kept with an adult at all times, and children should be supervised during their use. Instructions should be given for the best way of using tools—sitting down, with movements made away from the body, in the company of an adult. Sticks should be carried only if they are shorter than an arm's length. Longer sticks and firewood should be dragged into position. The frequency of insect bites and stings can be reduced if long sleeves are worn; everyone should be warned of the possibility of tick infestation and reminded that they should check themselves after an event involving long grass or meadowland.

At the end of an event, the group should ensure that the site is left clean and as safe as possible, and that non-biodegradable evidence of their presence has been removed. The safety leader should make a final inspection of the site before leaving.

Inevitably, craft activities involve some safety hazards, but it is the responsibility of the organisers to minimise them.

Adults should ensure that sharp knives and scissors are never left lying around and that any crafts using small objects that could be a choking hazard are continually supervised by adults. Try to keep the ratio of adults to children as high as possible for crafts that use small objects, or if seeds and berries are involved that look tempting to eat but are poisonous. Children's scissors and round-ended knives should be used where possible; if sharp tools are necessary, careful one-to-one supervision by an adult is desirable. When gathering objects from nature, be aware of brambles and stinging nettle patches, which could also hide hazards such as ditches or potholes. Do not leave branches or foliage in a condition that is hazardous for the next person who arrives at the place: for example, ensure that bramble branches are looped back in a secure fashion.

Edible crafts in any environment, but particularly in an outdoor situation, carry significant hygiene hazards, often caused by the tendency of young children to put everything in their mouths. Try to ensure that the edible crafting area is kept separate from other activity areas, and, if the site is particularly dirty or muddy, cover a polythene sheet with banqueting roll for cleanliness. This will also help with the clearing up afterwards, avoiding the possibility of encouraging rats and other vermin by leaving food debris at the site.

Keep a good supply of antibacterial hand wipes nearby and ensure that children have cleansed their hands with the wipes or with hand gel if there are no clean washing water facilities available. At the end of the session, children should be encouraged to clean their hands again to prevent food being spread about the site. Keep food crafting equipment separate from the other crafting and activity materials: an airtight plastic box can be used for transporting implements and utensils hygienically to and from the site.

Some of the edible crafts involve cooking, either over a fire or, as in the case of the bread rolls, in a domestic oven. Especial care should be taken over these activities, with fire safety rules being strictly followed.

Equipment and resources

Once you have established your venue, decide what sort of equipment you will need and where you are going to store it. You might find the list of suggested equipment and resources on pages 33–34 useful, but the requirements for each event will vary. Obviously, if there is on-site storage available, the number and complexity of activities you undertake can be greater than if every item of equipment has to be transported to and from each event.

As a minimum, you will need a carefully considered first aid kit (see 'Safety considerations, p. 24), but you may also want to have food and drinks facilities, or tools for building and maintaining a fire and other woodcraft activities. Small bug-hunting boxes can be purchased cheaply from craft and toy shops, but you may want to establish colonies of ants or worms in tanks for a short time. Access to water is important—essential for fire-related activities. Tarpaulins may be desirable for seating or shelter, although the environment must not be so heavily manipulated that the event ceases to have any relationship with the landscape and weather at all.

When your venue has been chosen, equipment collected and group gathered, do not hesitate to select the first appropriate occasion to hold an Outdoor Church event. Too much time spent on preparation can mean that the event is delayed almost indefinitely. Although safety should never be compromised, it is often better simply to set off and adapt as you go along, rather than continue to perfect something which, since it involves the unpredictability of the natural world, will never run exactly as planned.

Natural Crafts

As the focus for the crafts is on natural objects, the amount of equipment that you will need, in addition to what the outdoors can provide, is quite limited. However, it should be noted that some of the crafts require some indoor preparation. Do make sure, at the planning stage of your event, that the suggested craft is appropriate and does not require resources that are beyond the capacity of the group or the event. Otherwise, it might be a good idea to choose another craft from the same season, which makes fewer demands in terms of facilities or skill. When considering your event, take into account whether the craft is suitable for use outside or whether it might be more successfully created indoors. The event should be, above all, a relaxed, informal offering, rather than overly stressful owing to the quality of the craft produced or the technical challenges to be overcome.

The following is a list of the basic equipment that you will find useful, although the individual crafts will require additional materials. Encourage your group to collect 'junk' such as loo roll tubes and margarine and yoghurt pots; these can all be incorporated into the more free-flowing crafts.

All the materials and resources are easily available, either in shops such as Hobbycraft or in large supermarkets.

- Glue gun
- Washable PVA glue and spreaders
- Masking tape
- Sticky tape
- Acrylic paint in all colours
- Poster paint in all colours
- Paintbrushes, both thick and thin
- Lining paper (found in DIY shops, it is a very cheap way of providing paper for large-scale craft projects)
- Thin card in all colours (photocopiable card will save time if you want to print templates from the internet)
- Paper in all colours and patterns
- Pencils
- Felt pens or crayons
- Children's safety scissors
- String and wool

Photographs of the craft activities can be found at www.barnabasinchurches.org.uk/9780857464163.

Edible crafts

Here again, the ingredients will vary according to the individual crafts, but everything can be bought either from Hobbycraft or Lakeland (which both do a very good online order service) or a large supermarket.

- Blunt-ended knives for spreading
- Piping bags and icing nozzles of various sizes
- Children's rolling pins
- Plastic food bags
- Mixing bowls
- Cupcakes
- Buttercream icing in vanilla and chocolate
- Fondant icing in a variety of colours (you can buy white icing and mix your own colours, but supermarkets sell a large range of coloured icing, which makes things much easier and quicker)
- Digestive biscuits
- Oreo cookies
- Cake decorations such as gold and silver balls, licorice laces and so on
- Writing icing
- Marshmallows, large and small

Recipes

Many children suffer from one or more food allergies and intolerances, and one danger when working with very young children and food is that these allergies may not yet have manifested themselves. Nuts can provoke particularly severe reactions, even when being encountered for the first time, so there are no nuts or nut products used in any of these recipes except for the House on the Rock, which uses mini Battenberg cakes, containing almonds. These can be replaced with slices of plain cake, such as madeira.

Cupcakes

Although it may be quicker and simpler to buy your cupcakes (a dozen cost around £1 from most supermarkets), this recipe is very simple. It makes 24 cakes, but you can produce any number by multiplying up the ingredients.

Ingredients
- 120 g self-raising flour
- 120 g margarine or butter at room temperature
- 120 g caster sugar
- Two eggs
- 1 tsp baking powder

Pre-heat the oven to 180°C/Gas Mark 4. Line two 12-hole cupcake tins with paper cake cases.

Weigh all the ingredients into a large mixing bowl together and beat with an electric whisk. The mixture will gradually turn a paler colour and become light and fluffy. Check the consistency of the mix: if you lift a spoonful of it out of the bowl, the mixture should drop off the spoon slowly.

Put about a teaspoonful of cake batter into each paper cake case, then bake in the oven for about 10–12 minutes.

Check after ten minutes to see whether the cakes look light brown in colour. Test them by pushing gently with your finger on top of a cake. If it springs back and is firm to the touch, then the cakes are ready.

Once the cakes are cooked, take them out of the tins and let them cool on a wire rack.

Biscuits

Ingredients
- 200 g unsalted butter or margarine at room temperature
- 200 g caster sugar
- One beaten egg
- 400 g flour

Beat the sugar and butter together until the mixture lightens in colour and becomes smooth.

Gradually add the egg, continuing to beat. Add the flour, beating slowly until the ingredients start to come together into a lump. Bring the dough together into a ball with your hands, then wrap it in clingfilm and put it in the fridge for ten minutes.

Roll out the cooled dough between two sheets of baking paper, cut out your biscuit shapes and place them on lightly greased baking trays, then put them back into the fridge for another ten minutes.

Cook the biscuits at 160°C/Gas Mark 4 for about eight minutes or until light brown. Don't let them get too dark, as they will continue cooking on the tray for a few minutes after you have taken them out of the oven. Once the biscuits are cooked, keep them on the tray to harden for a minute or so, then transfer them to a wire rack to cool.

BEGINNING AND ENDING THE EVENT

Although each event will have a character of its own, and although creativity and spontaneity are a vital part of the uniqueness and excitement of Outdoor Church, it is useful to have a slightly more structured beginning and ending to each event, so that the themes can be introduced and any loose ends tied up. Each group should be able to inform the style and substance of these openings and closings, but below are some suggestions for possible inclusion.

Because the suggestions include responses for the congregation, you may wish to provide your community with service sheets or booklets. These should be as simple and brief as possible so that the spontaneity of a gathering is not overly restricted. It might also be worth laminating your service sheets, so that they can be used in all conditions. However, if this goes against the spirit of your event, the responses can be spoken by individuals or just by the event leader.

The responses that follow can be downloaded from www.barnabasinchurches.org.uk/9780857464163.

Beginning

Welcome and introductory prayer

This is the day that the Lord has made
Let us rejoice and be glad in it

Gracious God, who made the world and set the moon and the stars in the heavens, we praise and bless you for the wonders of your creation that surround us. Help us to be aware of your presence as we celebrate your glory, that we may share in your concern for all created things.

Confession

Be praised, my Lord, through those who forgive for love of you; through those who endure sickness and trial. We bring to mind those occasions when we have not spoken or acted as we should, and we pray for those people who have been hurt by our words and deeds.

Lord have mercy
Lord have mercy

We repent of those times when we have not cared for the creation as we ought, allowing it to be spoiled and damaged through our thoughtlessness.

Reproduced with permission from *Outdoor Church* by Sally Welch, published by Barnabas for Children, 2016. www.barnabasinchurches.org.uk

Christ have mercy
Christ have mercy

We are sorry that we have not valued ourselves as children of God, allowing negative thoughts and feelings to cause us to stumble on the path.

Lord have mercy
Lord have mercy

For all these things, we ask God's forgiveness through Christ whose love redeemed us all.

Thus says God, the Lord, who created the heavens and stretched them out, who spread out the earth and what comes from it, who gives breath to the people on it and spirit to those who walk in it: I am the Lord, I have called you in righteousness, I have taken you by the hand and kept you; I have given you as a covenant to the people, a light to the nations, to open the eyes that are blind, to bring out the prisoners from the dungeon, from the prison those who sit in darkness. I am the Lord, that is my name; my glory I give to no other. [Isaiah 42:5–8]

Worthy are you, our Lord and God, to receive glory and honour and power, for you created all things, and by your will they existed and were created. [Revelation 4:11]

Reproduced with permission from *Outdoor Church* by Sally Welch, published by Barnabas for Children, 2016. www.barnabasinchurches.org.uk

Ending

We gather at the end of our time together
Meeting together to rest in your peace

We rejoice in the evidence of God's love in creation, and for the opportunities to discover and learn that we have experienced. Through the wonders of the natural world, help us to discern God's glory.

For by him all things were created, in heaven and on earth, visible and invisible. All things were created through him and for him. [Colossians 1:16, ESV] For this we give thanks.

Here you could offer a short time for sharing discoveries and experiences, showing art works and constructions, and demonstrating new skills learned or old ones practised. This should be an occasion in which everyone can participate if they wish, encouraging all ages to contribute their achievements in an informal and affirming way.

We rejoice in the evidence of God's love in each other and in ourselves, and for the miracle that is our lives.

I praise you, for I am fearfully and wonderfully made. Wonderful are your works; my soul knows it very well. [Psalm 139:14, ESV]

Reproduced with permission from *Outdoor Church* by Sally Welch, published by Barnabas for Children, 2016. www.barnabasinchurches.org.uk

We commit ourselves to working together to care for God's creation and for our neighbours, that we may live in harmony with all.

Renew us in the spirit of our minds, that we may put on the new self, created after the likeness of God in true righteousness and holiness. [Ephesians 4:23–24]

In the beginning was the Word, and the Word was with God, and the Word was God. He was in the beginning with God. All things came into being through him, and without him not one thing came into being. What has come into being in him was life, and the life was the light of all people. The light shines in the darkness, and the darkness did not overcome it. [John 1:1–5]

Let us go in peace, for God makes known to us the path of life. In his presence there is fullness of joy; at his right hand are pleasures for evermore.

The grace of our Lord Jesus Christ, and the love of God, and the fellowship of the Holy Spirit, be with us all, ever more, Amen

Reproduced with permission from *Outdoor Church* by Sally Welch, published by Barnabas for Children, 2016. www.barnabasinchurches.org.uk

Parables and festivals:

Outdoor Church event suggestions and activities

Spring

Outdoor Church celebrates the season of spring by rejoicing in the signs of new growth that surround all of us. Even those who live in the most urban environments can be made aware of the slow green haze of tiny leaf buds appearing on trees, and of the sounds of birds as they call out to attract a mate. Listening activities focus on the different songs of birds and the challenge of trying to spot and identify the singer. Feathers shaken free during the preening process can be hunted and collected.

Although the days are getting longer, the weather is still unreliable and the activities take account of the possibility of a damp or even rainy environment; many of the suggested activities can be done in wet weather and none of them involve too much sitting or being still. Despite showers and breezes, though, the earth is beginning to warm up and prepare itself for the new time of planting. Deep beneath the surface of the soil, roots are stretching out and buried seeds begin to shoot and grow towards the warmth of the light. The green tops of bulbs can be seen poking through the leaf mould of last year's growth, and the circle of life begins once more. Now is the time to prepare the soil for new plants, digging and raking, clearing out weeds and stones, before carefully scattering seeds in neat rows or small holes, marking their place and protecting them from the ravages of birds, hungry from their singing, who seek an easy and nutritious meal.

The sower and the seed

'A farmer went out to sow some seed,' began Jesus. 'He took handfuls of seed, and cast it from side to side as he walked along.

'Some seed fell on the path. Birds came and quickly gobbled it up.

'Some seed fell on soil that was full of stones. The seed began to grow quite quickly, but it did not last long. Its roots had not stretched down deep into the soil so that when the sun beat down upon it, the plants shrivelled up and died.

'Some seed landed among thorns and as it grew up, it was choked by the thorns so it could not produce fruit.

'But some seed fell on good rich soil. There it began to grow, strong and healthy, until eventually it produced a good harvest.

'Listen well, and try to understand the message of the story.'

BARNABAS CHILDREN'S BIBLE, NO. 268 (MARK 4:3–9)

Reflecting on the story

The parables of Jesus are known for the surprises that are contained within them. They are stories that reverse expectation, turn away from the norm and bring in a new order of things, having turned the old order upside down.

The story of the sower and seed is no different, as it tells us something about the sheer generosity of the kingdom of heaven—a far cry from the traditional view of God as critic and judge. For who, if they had but a small amount of seed (precious in those days of hand-to-mouth existence, when every piece of grain was hoarded because it alone might stave off starvation), would treat it like the farmer does in this story? Who would go out one day and scatter seed where it could not possibly grow—among thorns, on dry ground, even on the path? True, the method of broadcasting meant that some seed inevitably went where it was not intended, but the wise farmer was careful to let this happen as little as possible. In this story, though, seed is being flung everywhere—and then the farmer's careless ways are rewarded, as the seed that does sprout produces a ridiculously large harvest.

Perhaps God is telling us not to be so careful with the gifts that we have, not to hoard them in a miserly fashion but to share with others the good things, the talents and the love we have been given. After all, we too may have seemed unlikely ground on which to sow. Perhaps our natures are prickly like thorns; perhaps there are places in our hearts that are like stones, cold and unloving. It is God's great generosity to us that has enabled us to flourish, and this generosity needs to be shared as we witness to our faith and God's love for all people. Some of our actions, our gifts, may well be unappreciated, but seed grows in the most unlikely places. Perhaps we will see signs of the kingdom flourish where we might never have expected them, in ways that exceed our wildest imaginings.

Activities

Preparation

We celebrate all things bird-like in these activities, so it is worth having a look for an area of land where there is evidence that birds have been nesting. Looking for birds that are eating seeds might also present a challenge, so it is a good idea to bring seed along with you. If you have time, you could visit your proposed feeding site a couple of days in advance and put food out so that the birds begin to view it as a safe feeding site. Pigeons are less fearful of human beings than other birds are, so an urban environment might even be an advantage here, as long as you bring a plentiful supply of food. There will be a feather hunt, and feathers may be quite hard to find, so you may want to gather a selection of different bird feathers beforehand.

Being, looking, listening

After the hard work of singing the dawn chorus, birds are hungry and will go in search of food. Any area of open ground is a suitable place to wait for birds to come and feed, and to watch them while they do. If you wish, you can bring different types of food and notice which type the birds prefer to eat. Most birds like sunflower seeds, with others preferring millet or crushed peanuts. Scatter the seeds some distance away from where you will be watching. Make sure everyone will be comfortable in their positions, as too much wriggling and noise will frighten the birds away. You might want to provide plastic sheeting or dustbin sacks to sit on if the ground is damp.

Encourage the group to be still and listen for the sounds of birds in the trees, and try to spot them in the branches as they look to see if it is safe to land and eat. Watch how the birds eat; notice whether they seem nervous or not and how easily startled they are. If it is later in the season, you might be lucky enough to see them carry the food away to feed their young; you might even spot the nest. Observe how the birds react to each other—whether they squabble over food, and how the smaller birds struggle to get food from the larger ones. See how different they all are: try to spot differences between two birds of the same species as well as noticing the differences between the various species.

COLLECTING: FEATHERS

Feathers are a vital piece of equipment for birds: feathers keep them warm, they attract mates, and they enable the bird to fly. Over time—from exposure to sunlight, rubbing against neighbouring feathers or branches, flying, or attack from parasites—feathers can wear out and need to be replaced. Moulting takes place at different times in different bird species, and many birds will have a new set of feathers for the breeding season, but a careful search of an area may reveal many more feathers than you expect.

Try to find different types of feather—the small, downy ones that help to trap air close to a bird's body to keep it warm, as well as the larger, sleek wing feathers with tiny hooks, which enable the feathers to stick together to become wind- and waterproof.

CREATING: BIRD MASKS

If you did not manage to collect many feathers, they can be purchased by the bagful from craft shops. The brightly coloured dyed ones are easier to source but not really appropriate for this activity. Try to find natural feathers; it is worth paying a bit extra for specific types, such as pheasant tail feathers, or you may end up with only the small, downy type for your activity.

If you can only find artificial colours, making a chick or duckling will not take you too far away from a natural look. Cut circles of yellow card for the head and body, and provide stick-on eyes, small orange triangles for beaks, and yellow feathers. You will need a fairly strong glue, such as washable PVA, to stick on the beak and feathers. If this takes too long to dry, then sticky tape may be an easier option.

With natural feathers, bird masks can be made by gluing feathers on to a card mask shape. These can be ordered pre-cut from craft suppliers or can be made more cheaply by cutting a paper plate in two and making eye holes where appropriate. If you only managed to find a few feathers, they could be stuck on to a cardboard headband, which can then be coloured or decorated according to inclination.

NB: Before using natural feathers for arts and crafts activities, they can be cleaned of possible mites or parasites by placing them in a clean pillowcase and putting them in a tumble dryer on full heat for half an hour. This should make them safe to use.

Feasting: chicks

You will need (per chick):
- One cupcake
- Buttercream icing
- Yellow or brown fondant icing
- Orange fondant icing or a jelly diamond
- Chocolate dots
- Circular cookie cutter, the size of the cupcake
- Leaf-shaped cookie cutter

It is probably best to cut out all the shapes beforehand, unless the children are old enough to roll out quite a lot of fondant icing.

From the yellow or brown icing, cut a circle to form the body, and two leaf shapes, which will form the wings.

Either cut a small triangular beak from the orange icing or cut the jelly diamond in half to make a beak.

Assemble the fondant shapes on the cake to look like a chick, and stick them on with buttercream icing. Add the chocolate dots for eyes.

It is quite important to have a ready-made example for this craft or it could get confusing.

Celebrating: bird spotting

Prepare yourself with camouflage clothing, binoculars and a good bird guide and try to find as many different types of bird as you can. Look for signs that birds have been present— feathers, broken eggshells, and nests in trees or hidden in hedgerows. Never disturb birds, particularly those that are nesting: the best place to watch birds is from a distance. If you cannot be outside, watching birds from a window can be just as interesting.

The more birds you spot, the better you will become at identifying them, but don't get too caught up in this process unless you can find an expert to help you. It's better simply to observe the way they fly and how they feed and interact with each other than to spend too much time looking them up in books.

The mustard seed

He told them another parable: 'The kingdom of heaven is like a mustard seed, which a man took and planted in his field. Though it is the smallest of all seeds, yet when it grows, it is the largest of garden plants and becomes a tree, so that the birds come and perch in its branches.'

MATTHEW 13:31–32 (NIV)

Reflecting on the story

One of my favourite memories is of fetching my youngest child from school and taking him, because it was a sunny day, to the park to play. When he got to the park and saw that huge green space just waiting for him to play in, he was so thrilled that he lay down and rolled in it, just like any young animal. I looked at that joy, that sheer delight in life, and I marvelled. It is such a gift to be able to see the world as it is, without the lenses we so often wear of disappointment, low expectation and negativity.

The parable of the mustard seed reminds us that we must not ignore the smallest signs of God's kingdom, but must search for them expectantly. When we find them, as we will, we must rejoice in them. We should not give up on them, despite the brokenness of the world around us, but should believe in the possibilities of God, however small they seem.

There is a story about one of the winners of the Nobel Peace Prize, Mother Teresa of Calcutta. Her whole work began with a vision, which she shared with her superiors at the convent where she lived. She told them, 'I have three pennies and a dream from God to build an orphanage.' Those in charge reminded her gently that with only three pennies she would surely achieve nothing: these were true mustard seed resources. But Mother Teresa simply smiled and replied that with God and three pennies she could do anything.

The parable of the mustard seed reminds us that God's beginnings may be small, but his results are great. Our task is to look at the world around us for the signs of the kingdom, which may be no larger than a mustard seed, and, when we have spotted them, to share them with others with love and delight.

Activities

Preparation

This session focuses on looking at things in a new way, so little is needed by way of resources. The collecting activity includes the option of making a journey stick from the things that have been collected. If you are planning a trip around a wooded area, finding enough sticks for this activity should not be a problem, but otherwise you might find it helpful to collect some stout sticks or garden canes, and bring some brightly coloured wool or string.

Being, looking, listening

Find a clear space in which to stand or a comfortable place to sit and look around you. Try to imagine that you are a stranger to this planet, looking at things for the first time, without knowing what they are. What patterns can you spot in your surroundings? You might want to look upwards at a tree and notice the patterns that the branches make against the sky. The sky itself may be patterned with clouds or spotted with birds or aeroplanes. If you are in a built-up area, look at the skyline of the buildings and telegraph poles.

Look down at the ground. Watch how the sunlight makes shapes on the ground as shadows change and grow. Perhaps last year's dead leaves have been swept into a circle by the wind, or twigs have fallen to the ground in a particular way. Does the grass grow in a particular pattern?

Find one object, such as a stone or a plant, and examine it very closely. Look at the patterns made on its surface, the shadows and shapes. Are any the same? Can you spot any similarities between objects?

Collecting: sticks and natural objects

If you want to make a journey stick, you will need to find a good-sized stick to form your base. It should be long enough to hold everything you want, but not too big to carry: about 50 cm is a good length.

When you have done that, or if you decide to make a picture frame, go for a walk and collect things that will remind you of the day. They could be objects on which you've noticed an interesting pattern, such as an attractively patterned stone, or one of an unusual colour. They could be signs of new life, such as a twig with buds or new leaves on it. They could be more abstract reminders or simply natural things that you think are beautiful. Make sure they are not too big or they will dominate your craft, and remember that if they are living things, such as young leaves or flowers, they will fade and die away from their habitat.

CREATING: JOURNEY STICK OR PICTURE FRAME

When you have collected enough objects, attach them to your journey stick by wrapping them to the stick with wool or string. Use one long piece of wool or attach further bits as you go. The wool can be brightly coloured or plain, and you can add other objects if you wish, such as beads or sequins.

For a picture frame, you can either order plain cardboard or wooden frames from a craft supplier or make your own by cutting out the centre from a rectangle of card. Stick your objects to the frame with a good strong glue: washable PVA or tacky glue is best. Alternatively, you can wrap the objects on to the frame with wool, so that the frame is completely covered.

FEASTING: A MUSTARD TREE

You will need (per tree):
- One large handful of popcorn
- 1 tbsp green candy melts
- Digestive biscuit or similar
- Yellow writing icing (optional)

If you have a popcorn maker, the teaching can be made even more visual, as you will show how just a small handful of corn turns into a whole bucketful. If not, you can buy microwaveable popcorn, which you can prepare beforehand.

Melt the candy melts either in a microwave on medium heat in 20-second bursts, stirring each time, or in a bowl over boiling water, being mindful of the risk of scalding. When the melts are runny, add the popcorn and stir carefully until it is covered with the candy.

Using (clean) hands, scoop up a handful of popcorn and quickly mould it into a tree shape before placing it on the biscuit to set. If you want to decorate your tree when it is solid, you can use yellow writing icing to make mustard flowers.

Celebrating: trail making

Make a trail leading the group from its assembly point either to the outside area or back to the worship space.

A small group walks on ahead of the main congregation and shows them which direction to follow, with signs laid on the ground or attached to trees. Make sure the signs are either biodegradable, such as sticks and grass, or removed as soon as the activity is over. You can use laminated paper arrows if necessary, but encourage the group to search for suitable organic material with which to make the signs.

- A straight arrow indicates the direction to walk in.
- An arrow that bends in the middle, at 90 degrees to the right or left, shows where a turn is to be taken.
- A cross means that this is not the correct path.

- A square with an arrow at one side and a number inside the square indicates that a hidden message can be found: followers need to walk in the direction of the arrow, for the number of paces shown in the square.

- Three perpendicular sticks or rows of stones means danger.

- A large circle with a smaller circle inside it indicates the end of the trail.

Treasure in the field

'Imagine that there is some treasure hidden in a field. One day, a man accidentally finds the treasure. He buries it again quickly, then goes back home. He sells his home, his furniture, his cooking pots—even his donkey—so that he can buy the field. Then the treasure is his, and nothing could be worth more than that.'

The people listened. Some of them understood. Jesus meant that God's kingdom was more valuable than anything they owned. It was worth doing anything to be part of it.

BARNABAS CHILDREN'S BIBLE, NO. 269 (MATTHEW 13:44)

Reflecting on the story

It is sometimes easy simply to sit back and enjoy the parables of Jesus for their own sake, and the story of buried treasure that is found by accident is one that appeals to everyone who enjoys the idea of being surprised by unexpected gifts. However, it is not enough simply to enjoy the word of God, the treasure in the field. We have to seek it actively, to allow its teachings to become part of our hearts and minds and souls. We need to burn with the desire to understand, to fulfil our potential, to risk losing everything in a gamble to attain the immeasurable prize.

The kingdom of God is shown here to be more than just a noun. It is a verb, an action, and it does not come alive until we enter into it. It is not enough that we merely appreciate the treasure in its field; we must respond to its call, act on its challenge and let it enter and change our lives. We are being offered—all of us, free of charge—a share of God's infinite love, a place in his glorious kingdom. We need only to reach out and make it ours.

Activities

Preparation

This session is all about seeking and looking. Ideally, the group should be able to observe the movements of ants, so it is worth spending some time looking for an anthill or nest nearby. The most common place to find them is in the ground, but looking under or inside logs might be useful. Ants like dry earth around plant roots, so look around the bottom of trees. They are also attracted to sandy soil, so, in an urban environment, look in piles of sand.

Being, looking, listening

Throughout the long winter months, colonies of ants have struggled to survive, often travelling quite some distance to find food for the queen ant and the newly hatched grubs. If you find an ant nest, do not disturb it by going too close; instead, watch how the ants move to and from it. Occasionally they will stop and appear to communicate with each other. Often, they will follow each other in long lines, picking up a sweet scent that has been laid by other ants so that they can find their way to a food source and then back home to the anthill.

Watch how busy they are and how quickly they move. If you place a crumb of food in their path, see how they examine it and decide whether or not they can carry it. If the crumb is big, two or three ants might carry it together back to the anthill.

If you cannot find an anthill or ants, why not make a tiny trail for ants to follow? Draw out a path for an ant using a stick on the ground. Try to have an 'ant's eye view' of obstacles and take your trail round any large or difficult-to-climb objects.

Collecting: shaking a tree

Take a large baking tray and line it with white paper. Place the tray on the ground directly under a small tree or a large branch of a tree, or hold the tray as level as you can. For larger events, use a white sheet and either lay it on the ground or ask a number of people to stand around the tree trunk, holding the sheet.

Shake the tree or branch as vigorously as you can, taking care to do no actual damage to the tree. Then have a look to see what has been gathered. There might be small twigs, leaves, insects and old seeds. Take care that any insects that have been shaken loose are treated gently and released near their tree or on a branch. Carefully collect up the non-living objects for your craft.

Creating: a display shelf

Make a display of the things you collected from the tree. You will need three toilet paper tubes and an A4 piece of stiff card. Cut the tubes into smaller tubes, each about 3 or 4 cm high, so that you have seven in total. Paint them tree green.

While the tubes are drying, paint a landscape on your A4 card, with a single large tree trunk in the middle of the picture. When the tubes are dry, glue them together into a 'beehive' formation on the cardboard, at the top of the tree trunk you have painted. There should be a top line of two tubes, a middle line of three, then a bottom line of two, to look like the top part of the tree.

Pin your display shelves up, then carefully place in them the objects that you found.

Feasting: a treasure chest

You will need (per chest):
- One cupcake
- 1 dsp chocolate buttercream icing
- One Oreo cookie with filling removed
- One small chocolate-covered mini roll (half the size of the usual mini roll).
- Small sugar cake decorations, such as gold and silver balls
- Gold, silver or white writing icing
- A knife for spreading
- A small food bag
- Children's rolling pin

If you cannot source the small mini rolls (I know of only one major supermarket that sells them), use ordinary non-chocolate-coated mini rolls cut in two.

Before the activity, slice a small wedge of cake from the length of the mini roll so that it looks like a half-opened treasure chest. I have experimented with cutting them in half and then wedging them open, but the chocolate tends to crack and small hands cannot balance the two halves easily.

If you are short of time, crush the Oreo cookies before-hand. Bear in mind, though, that this can be an enjoyable part of the activity.

Spread the cupcake with the chocolate buttercream icing.

Place the biscuits in the food bag and hit the bag gently with a rolling pin until the biscuits become crumbs. Sprinkle the crumbs on the cupcake to look like an earthy field.

Spread a small amount of chocolate icing in the wedge-shaped gap of the mini roll, then fill the rest of the gap with gold and silver balls. It does not matter if some fall out; there can be overspill on to the soil.

Place the mini roll on to the cupcake. Use the writing icing to create locks, hinges and so on, according to the skill of the crafter.

Celebrating: an obstacle course

Make an obstacle course, using anything you can find to challenge the skills or balance of the group. Invite people in the group to be in charge of one obstacle each, or, if the group is smaller, join together for all of them.

Obstacles can involve climbing under low branches, walking along tree trunks, leaping puddles and scrambling over rocks. If your open space is a park, the obstacles can be challenges, such as doing five star jumps or a three-legged race. Your obstacle course could contain mental challenges too, such as naming five animals to be found in the Bible or three of Joseph's brothers.

Keep in mind the safety requirements of your group so that the activity does not become too challenging.

Growing seed

[Jesus] also said, 'This is what the kingdom of God is like. A man scatters seed on the ground. Night and day, whether he sleeps or gets up, the seed sprouts and grows, though he does not know how. All by itself the soil produces corn—first the stalk, then the ear, then the full grain in the ear. As soon as the corn is ripe, he puts the sickle to it, because the harvest has come.'

MARK 4:26–29 (NIV)

Reflecting on the story

There will be times in everyone's lives when things seem very dark and almost hopeless. Either through our own actions or because of events that are beyond our control, it can seem as if the light in our lives has dimmed or even gone out completely. But even in the middle of that dark night of the soul, the seeds of new growth are sprouting. Shoots of hope, of renewed faith and of love are reaching out of the blackness to burst forth in glorious, often unexpected ways.

The sower scatters his seed in all sorts of places, for reasons we cannot understand. Again, beyond our comprehension, the seed falls to the ground and buries itself. It seems as if nothing has changed, nothing has had an effect. But deep beneath the surface, new life is being created and will soon be visible to all.

We do not understand the ways of God; we must simply believe and trust in his eternal love and look diligently for the seeds of his kingdom wherever they sprout. Just as most seeds need darkness to begin their lives, so times of darkness can be fruitful in our own lives.

We too can be part of the sowing, as small acts of kindness, gestures of love and friendship are the seeds of a God-filled community, caring for each other and the wider world in small ways. The poet Christina Rossetti wrote, 'Give us grace, O Lord, to work while it is day, fulfilling diligently and patiently whatever duty thou appointest us, doing small things in the day of small things and great labours if thou summonest us to any.'

Activities

Preparation

This session focuses on looking for signs of new growth and hope. Participants are encouraged to hunt for things that a bird might use to build a nest, so it will be useful if you have already collected a few examples to show them. In urban, built-up areas, the search will be challenging, but this only serves to demonstrate how hard it must be for birds. Parallels can be drawn with those people whose search for hope in their lives is long and difficult.

Being, looking, listening

In the spring, the dawn chorus begins again after the long silence of winter, as birds begin their annual search for a mate and try to defend their territory from other birds. When it is still dark, before even the first signs of light, you can hear the songs of birds echoing from the trees. Though few at first, the sounds increase in number and variety as more and more birds join in, until the full light of day brings an end to the joyful noise.

Most birds stop singing as the daylight gets brighter, for fear of attracting predators, and also because they need to search for food. However, if your group is very still, the sounds of birds can be heard almost anywhere in the British Isles and at any time of day. Although it is interesting if the birds can be identified, all that is necessary is to listen to the sounds they make. Focus your entire attention on listening and appreciate the incredible richness and variety of sounds that are produced. You should be able to distinguish the different birdsongs, even though spotting the bird that is singing is often very challenging.

Collecting: materials for a bird's nest

Try to find as many different things as possible that a bird might use to build a nest. There are the traditional materials, such as small twigs, moss, lichen and soft feathers, but more unusual items might also be included. Different birds use different materials: blackbirds use mud to stiffen their nests of woven grass and twigs, while other birds use moss and feathers to line holes in trees and other places.

When you have collected a heap of useful material, leave it where birds might be able to make use of it, taking care not to make the site untidy.

Creating: growing cress

Cress seeds are wonderfully quick and easy to grow and demonstrate the cycle of planting, nurturing and harvest in a short space of time. Seeds can be sprinkled on damp balls of cotton wool placed in egg boxes, or more elaborate constructions can be made using empty eggshells filled with either fine compost or cotton wool. The eggshells can be decorated to look like faces, with the cress producing a fine head of green 'hair'.

Feasting: an edible compost heap

You will need (per heap):

- One cupcake
- 2 tbsp chocolate buttercream icing
- Three Oreo cookies with filling removed
- Small amounts of fondant icing in different colours
- Jelly worms
- Knife for spreading
- Plastic food bag
- Rolling pin
- Paper plate

Crush the Oreo cookies by placing them in a food bag and rolling them with a rolling pin. (If the children are small or time is limited, you might want to crush the cookies beforehand.)

Take the cupcake out of its wrapper and place it upside down on the plate. Cover the cake with chocolate icing, quite roughly, so that it looks like a heap of soil. Scatter crushed cookie crumbs over the top of the icing.

With the fondant icing, make scraps of 'food' and place them on the compost heap. The scraps could include lettuce leaves, potato peelings and orange peel: try to choose objects of many different colours. Top with a jelly worm or make one from pink and brown fondant icing.

Celebrating: rainy-day activities

It would be too much to ask for every Outdoor Church event to take place in glorious sunshine, and inevitably there will be occasions when rain interferes with plans. However, this can be a useful metaphor for overcoming difficult or disappointing times in life, as well as reminding us that plants need rain as well as sunshine to grow. If possible, the outdoor event should take place anyway, with waterproofs, wellies and umbrellas to hand. Games such as jumping over puddles, jumping in puddles, catching raindrops and fashioning leaf and branch umbrellas will encourage participation in rainy-day worship.

If the weather is too bad or the group too vulnerable, watch raindrops race down window panes or build a rain gauge from a plastic carton to place outside and measure just how much water has fallen. These activities will help to focus on the advantages of wet weather.

Spring celebration: Rogation

God looked at everything he had made and saw that it was good. Then God made man and woman. He put them in charge of his creation, to care for it and cultivate it for food. God loved the people he had made and he saw that everything he had made was very good. Then God rested.

God gave Adam and Eve a beautiful garden to live in. It was full of plants and trees with fruit they could eat. The garden was watered by a river that ran through it and Adam and Eve tended the garden and worked in it. Adam and Eve were good company for each other. They shared the work and they lived happily together.

BARNABAS CHILDREN'S BIBLE, NOS. 1 AND 2 (GENESIS 1:26—2:15)

Reflecting on the story

In this, the story of the creation of the world and the part that human beings play within the creation (Genesis 1—2), we find the essential elements of our relationship with God and with his creation. Human beings were made in the image of God, to care for his world and to cultivate it for food. Although they had stewardship over the land and its harvests, this was to be a wise and provident stewardship, taking care not to abuse the land or corrupt it. The Genesis story reminds us that we are responsible for our world and that our relationship with it is one of mutuality and oversight, not aggressive exploitation. We are offered an opportunity to reflect on the beauty of the land that God has given us and to pray for its continued well-being.

It is believed that the festival of Rogationtide first made its way to the British Isles in the seventh century. It was essentially a time to ask God's blessing on the spring planting and pray for good weather and a bountiful harvest. Gradually, the festival became the occasion for 'beating the bounds'—that is, for the parish priest and congregation to walk around the boundaries of a parish, marking them out in a way that settled border and land disputes. In an Outdoor Church context, this celebration can be a way of reflecting on the wide variety of landscapes that surround us and the wonderful variety of plants and trees that, after the cold of winter, are beginning to show signs of new life.

Activities

Preparation

This session invites the group to explore as wide a variety of landscapes as possible. One way of doing this is to arrange a walk around the parish, taking in green spaces, water, built-up areas and trees or woods if possible. It is best to plan beforehand where you will lead your group, taking into consideration their age and mobility as well as any safety factors such as busy road crossings.

The celebration at the end involves creating a labyrinth. This can be done using the material available in a landscape, such as sticks, leaves and stones. Collecting this material is part of the celebration, but you might want to ensure that enough material is available in the site you have chosen. If you have access only to parkland, a labyrinth can be traced using flour or sawdust, both of which will need to be provided beforehand. For a celebration taking place within a building, the pattern can be marked out on the floor using chalk or masking tape.

Being, looking, listening

Go for a walk around your local environment, trying to include as many different landscapes as possible. Ask the group to walk quietly, listening for the different sounds in each landscape. Move slowly and gently, taking time to look carefully at everything you see. As you walk slowly through landscapes that have become familiar through constant sight, try to look at them with different eyes—eyes that are prepared to see the signs of God's glory in creation. Walk in a spirit of thankfulness for the range of blessings to be found in the scenery that surrounds you. Try to be aware of the immediacy of the environment and of the presence of God, enjoying his company, surrounded by evidence of his love.

As you walk past fields or gardens, look for signs of spring growth—the first flowers, buds on trees, and the green 'mist' on brown fields that signals the growth of the young crops. Ask God to bless this growth, and pray for those who cultivate the land.

Collecting: looking for signs of new growth

As you walk, collect signs of new life from the landscape—

twigs with buds or catkins, spring flowers and small shoots of new grass. Try to find as many different types as possible. Without damaging the plant too much, it might be possible to pick just one example of each sign of new life to take home and cherish. Be careful to leave enough so that the plant can still flourish and others can benefit from signs of spring.

CREATING: A LANDSCAPE

Create a landscape using handprints. Paint pads for hand-prints can be purchased from craft stores, or you can soak cleaning sponges in paint and place them on plates for people to use. Provide different shades of green and brown as well as flower colours. It might encourage nervous participants if you draw some outline shapes of hills, trees and flowers that can be filled in by handprints. Use fingerprints for flower petals and tree blossom, and build up a picture from everyone's contributions.

Alternatively, give each person a square piece of brown paper and ask them to make fingerprint shoots of corn or small flowers. These prints can then be taped together to form a large patchwork of spring fields.

FEASTING: FLOWER POT

You will need (per pot):
- Half a packet of chocolate-flavoured instant dessert powder
- 150 ml milk
- One small, flat-bottomed ice cream cone
- One Oreo cookie with filling removed

- Sprig of mint or basil, or edible flowers
- Small bowl
- Fork and spoon
- Plastic food bag
- Rolling pin
- Paper plate

Primroses are edible and make the flower pot look authentic, but you need to consider whether it is wise to use them, in case you give the impression that every garden flower is edible.

If you have small children or limited time, you might want to crush the cookies beforehand.

Mix the dessert powder and milk together, whisking until the mixture has thickened. Spoon it carefully into the ice cream cone, levelling the top.

Crush the Oreo cookies by putting them in a plastic food bag and rolling them until they look like soil. Sprinkle the crushed cookies on top of the chocolate mixture. 'Plant' the top with edible herbs or flowers.

Celebrating: building a labyrinth

Build a labyrinth, either by tracing the design in sand or soil with a stick or by gathering materials and building small walls with sticks, leaves, stones and so on. If the location is not suitable for this, the design can be traced in flour or marked out with chalk or masking tape. However, if possible, the act of gathering the material and building the labyrinth should be as much part of the activity as walking it afterwards.

The simplest pattern is the three-circuit classical design. Begin by drawing a cross in the centre of your space. Then place four dots in a square shape between the arms of the cross (fig. 1).

Fig. 1

The centre of the labyrinth is made by drawing an arc to connect the top arm of the cross with the dot to its right (fig. 2).

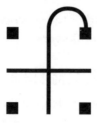

Fig. 2

The dot to the left of the top arm is then joined to the right-hand arm of the cross, sweeping round clockwise, over the top of the first arc (fig. 3).

Fig. 3

The left-hand arm of the cross is then joined to the dot below the right-hand arm of the cross (fig. 4).

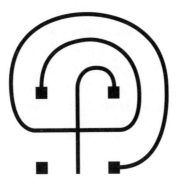

Fig. 4

Finally, the remaining dot is joined to the bottom arm of the cross (fig. 5). The walker enters at the bottom, on the left-hand side.

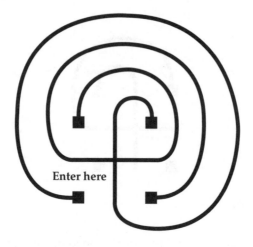

Enter here

Fig. 5

The size of your labyrinth depends on the amount of space you have to draw it in. Try to ensure that the paths are of equal widths and wide enough to walk along comfortably. If you can, leave a larger space in the centre for meditation and reflection, once the walker has arrived there.

Summer

The summer season brings a different set of opportunities for engaging with the natural world. In an environment that may be warmer and dryer than the spring, there can be a more relaxed feeling about planning events, hopeful that a rainy-day alternative won't be needed. The time spent outdoors, particularly with younger children, can lengthen, and occasions simply for resting and reflecting are more easy to arrange. The huge variety of wildlife that surrounds us even in the most urban of environments can be encountered on bug hunts and animal-tracking excursions, while the range of plants and flowers is also at its widest and most exuberant.

Through reflection, activities, exploring and simply being, we can explore God's call to us as part of his creation. The parables for the summer months look at the ways in which we should behave if we are to grow in our relationships with God and our neighbour. They offer a view of the world that is Christ-centred and people-focused. The brittle nature of material values and worldly success is revealed and a new way of being is illustrated through story and metaphor. We are invited to set our hearts and minds on God and, through doing so, to cherish the people with whom we live our lives and the environments in which these interactions take place. By physically entering into these stories, by engaging with the natural world in a loving, attentive way, we can understand more about the way God wants us to enjoy his creation and share it with others.

The good Samaritan

'But who is my neighbour?' asked the man.

'I will tell you a story,' said Jesus. 'There was once a man who was walking on the lonely road from Jerusalem to Jericho. He was attacked by some robbers, who stole his money and took his clothes and left him half dead by the side of the road.

'Later on, a priest came along the same road. He saw the injured man, but decided not to help him. He walked past on the other side.

'Some time later, a Levite came along the road. He also saw the wounded man, but did not stop to help.

'Finally, a Samaritan came along the road. As soon as he saw the man lying there, he stopped. He bandaged his wounds, he helped him on to his own donkey, and took him to an inn. He gave the innkeeper some money, and asked him to look after the injured man till he was well again. "When I return I will give you any more money you need," he said.'

Then Jesus asked the man who was listening to the story: 'Who was a good neighbour to the wounded man?'

'The one who helped him,' said the man.

'You must do the same as him,' said Jesus.

BARNABAS CHILDREN'S BIBLE, NO. 279 (LUKE 10:25–37)

Reflecting on the story

'Who is my neighbour?' Just before this passage, a man has asked Jesus what he must do to obtain eternal life. He must love his neighbour, Jesus replies, to which the man responds with that famous question. But I wonder if, rather than 'Who is my neighbour?' he is actually asking, 'Who is *not* my neighbour?' Perhaps the man wants to know where he can draw the line between the people he needs to help and the people he does not have to bother with. Maybe he seeks to know not just what he must do to obtain eternal life, but what the minimum requirements are for doing so.

This is quite an understandable reaction and one that we ourselves might share: how can we get what we want or need with the smallest amount of effort? Who are the people who do not have to be cared for? Who can safely be ignored? Perhaps the man had some ideas in his mind— thieves, vagrants, people with leprosy, all those rejected by mainstream society, those whom the man might think are unworthy of eternal life themselves.

Jesus' parable jolts both the man and the contemporary hearer of the story back to the reality of the Christian life. Everyone is our neighbour; we have a duty of care towards our families and our physical neighbours, but also towards those living further afield who are affected by our actions. Those people include farmers who struggle to fulfil milk quotas at punitive prices, children working in factories to produce goods cheaply so that we can overpurchase, and those affected by deforestation programmes that ruin local economies and alter the global climate. We have many neighbours; none of them can be ignored.

Activities

Preparation

This session has as its focus the interrelatedness of all people. We all have a responsibility for each other, however distantly connected we appear to be. It also asks us to reflect on the way that the things we do in our part of the world affect those who live elsewhere, either for good or ill. Our love for our fellow human beings flows from our love for God, which finds its natural outpouring in caring for each other as we ourselves are loved.

Being, looking, listening

First, find your open space. For this activity, no particular type of landscape is necessary, but it needs to be open and relatively quiet. Try to find somewhere that is as far from the noise of traffic and other distractions as possible.

Ask the group to spread out, far enough apart that they are not aware of anyone else, then to make themselves comfortable on the spot they have chosen. The activity can be done standing up or sitting, depending on the preference of the group.

Take a little time to get comfortable, then simply be still for a few moments. Allow the muscles of the body to relax. Let the tension disappear from jaw, neck, shoulders and back—wherever seems to be holding stress or fatigue. Breathe slowly, listening for the sounds of your breath as it goes in and out of your body. Listen to the other sounds your body is making. Perhaps your stomach is rumbling, your joints are creaking or your nose is sniffing. Allow these sounds to stay in your conscious thoughts and focus on them. Try not to be distracted by other thoughts that may come into your mind, but simply listen to the steady intake and expiration of breath, which continues all the time, whether you are aware of it or not.

Collecting: plants used to make dyes

Gather materials that can be used to make natural dyes. You may find some wild strawberries or cherries, elderberries or early blackberries, which are the most obvious materials, but many other plants can be used. Dandelion roots, crabapple bark, Queen Anne's lace and acorns will all make good dyeing materials.

You will need quite large amounts of dyeing material, so make sure you choose something that is present in abundance. If you don't find enough outside, onion skins, coffee grounds, red cabbage leaves and butternut squash rind are all effective dyes.

Creating: a tie-dye scarf or t-shirt

To make natural dyes, chop the gathered material into small pieces and place them in a large, old pot with twice as much water as material. If you add two cups of material, for example, put in four cupfuls of water. Bring to the boil and simmer, taking care not to let the pan boil dry. The longer you let the materials boil, the stronger the dye will be. After at least an hour, strain off the materials and keep the liquid.

Next, prepare your fabric for the dyeing process. Natural fabrics such as cotton tea towels, large handkerchiefs or T-shirts are ideal. If you are using berries, add half a cup of salt to eight cups of cold water, allow to dissolve, then soak the fabric in it for at least an hour. If you are using other materials, add one cup of vinegar to four cups of cold water and soak the fabric for at least an hour. Then place your wet fabric in the dyeing solution and bring to the boil once more. Allow to simmer for at least one hour, or longer for a stronger colour. (This part of the process could run in parallel with other activities, provided that it is properly supervised. Alternatively, it could be completed after the event.)

If you like, you can tie up parts of your fabric with elastic bands. These tightly bound areas of fabric will not get any dye, so will come out with a ring-shaped pattern.

When the dyeing process has come to an end, extract the fabric and rinse in cold water. Allow to dry naturally.

Feasting: bandaged people

You will need (per person to be made):
- One biscuit person (or biscuit-making ingredients)
- Writing icing in blue, red and black
- White fondant icing
- Coloured fondant icing (optional)
- Rolling pin and knife
- Paper plate

Many large supermarkets will supply people-shaped biscuits. It is best if you can find those that are completely undecorated, but, if they come with features, these can always be embellished. Alternatively, you can make your own biscuits using the recipe on page 36.

Use writing icing to give the person some features and hair. Older children might like to use coloured fondant icing to make simple robes for their people. Then roll out the white fondant icing and cut it into long strips, about 1 cm wide. Decide which part of your biscuit person has been injured and wrap the icing strips around it, as a bandage.

Celebrating: taking a walk, barefoot

Go for a barefoot walk. This activity might need some preparation, as it is a good idea to scout out the best place for it beforehand. If you have a regular meeting place for your Outdoor Church, make sure it is suitable for a barefoot walk: some urban outdoor areas are not safe because of animal mess, broken glass or other litter. If you can, choose a place with as many different textures as possible— mud, some bare soil, a stony path, smooth grass, logs and small sticks. However, even a park will offer footpaths, grass, playgrounds and probably a muddy patch near the football pitch. Make sure you bring towels for cleaning feet afterwards.

If you need to hold the event inside, lay out a series of potting trays containing different substances. These are big enough for adult feet, although you will need quite a lot of trays to avoid long queues. Trays have the advantage of offering a wide range of barefoot experiences—for example, jelly, cooked spaghetti, rice, seeds and oats, as well as sand, mud, water and possibly turf. Provide some bowls of water and towels for washing afterwards, and make sure the area around the trays is protected. If you place wet trays on towelling, this will prevent the area from becoming slippery.

Encourage everyone to experience as many sensations as possible and not to worry about getting wet or dirty feet. Walk slowly, feeling the differences between the various surfaces, allowing the mud to squish between your toes, feeling sand trickle over your feet and letting waves of water wash over your toes. Celebrate the many different sensations that you feel, just with one, often neglected, part of your body.

The talents

'For it will be like a man going on a journey, who called his servants and entrusted to them his property. To one he gave five talents, to another two, to another one, to each according to his ability. Then he went away. He who had received the five talents went at once and traded with them, and he made five talents more. So also he who had the two talents made two talents more. But he who had received the one talent went and dug in the ground and hid his master's money. Now after a long time the master of those servants came and settled accounts with them. And he who had received the five talents came forward, bringing five talents more, saying, "Master, you delivered to me five talents; here I have made five talents more." His master said to him, "Well done, good and faithful servant. You have been faithful over a little; I will set you over much. Enter into the joy of your master." And he also who had the two talents came forward, saying, "Master, you delivered to me two talents; here I have made two talents more." His master said to him, "Well done, good and faithful servant. You have been faithful over a little; I will set you over much. Enter into the joy of your master." He also who had received the one talent came forward, saying, "Master, I knew you to be a hard man, reaping where you did not sow, and gathering where you scattered no seed, so I was afraid, and I went and hid your talent in the ground. Here you have what is yours." But his master answered him, "You wicked and slothful servant! You knew that I reap where I have not sown and gather where I scattered no seed? Then you ought to have invested my money with the bankers, and at my coming I should have received what was my own with interest. So take the talent from him and give it to him who has the ten talents."'

MATTHEW 25:14–28 (ESV)

REFLECTING ON THE STORY

This story seems to be a straightforward account of the way God will judge the world at the end times. As usual, it takes an ordinary situation, common in New Testament times— in this case, of a man going on a journey and leaving his estate in the care of others. The caretakers who work hard at their task are rewarded, while those who do not are not. The message could thus be read simply as 'If you don't use what God has given you, he will take it all away and punish you.'

The danger of this interpretation is that it can suggest that the work we do for God will be judged on its quantity or quality, or both, and our fate decided accordingly. This ignores the fact that it is by grace that we are saved, not by works, as Paul tells us (Ephesians 2:8). So why is the servant who buries his talent punished? Perhaps the reason lies in the answer he gave when challenged by the master: 'I knew you to be a hard man, reaping where you did not sow, and gathering where you scattered no seed, so I was afraid, and I went and hid your talent in the ground. Here you have what is yours.' The master is angry not because the servant failed to multiply what had been given to him, but because he was afraid to try. He denied any responsibility for what he had been given and ignored it all.

So, too, we need to resolve not to be afraid to fail, but to use the gifts that God has given us to the best of our ability. Whether we succeed or fail is not as important as the effort we make, to work with what we have been given for the benefit of ourselves, our neighbours and the world around us, returning our blessings as best we can to the one who first blessed us.

Activities

Preparation

In this session, all things watery are encountered and explored. Ideally this session would take place near a river or lake or by the sea. However, if you are not able to do this, even a large puddle will do! Failing the presence of a natural puddle, one can be created.

As with all activities involving water, be aware of the risks. Keep away from steep or slippery riversides and ensure that small children are closely watched (see 'Safety considerations', page 23).

Being, looking, listening

Stand by the edge of an area of water and spend some time looking at the patterns that are made upon its surface. If the water is moving, see how the waves follow one another and the way they tumble and splash, noticing the water droplets that are hurled up into the sky. If the water is still, notice how the slightest amount of wind ripples the surface, changing the way the water looks as it moves, then settles slowly back into stillness. Observe the reflections of objects and how the movement of the water fragments these images. Notice how the sunlight is caught and reflected back in a thousand jewels of light. Look at the effect of the water on the riverbank or seashore, the patterns that are made by waves and ripples. See how the movement of the water also moves the earth and sand, so that it is constantly shifting and changing.

If you can do so safely, put your hand into the water and notice the effect this has on the water's movement. Feel the cold of the water against your skin, and look at the way any movement sends patterns across the surface.

Collecting: twigs and leaves

Find as many different types of twigs and leaves as you can. You will be using some of this material to make a raft, so be aware of the size of the raft you are going to build. Be careful not to damage the trees and plants you are collecting from, and make sure that you do not gather twigs or leaves from poisonous trees (see 'Safety considerations', page 23).

Creating: a wooden raft

Build a raft using the twigs and leaves you have gathered. Before you build, take account of the water in which you will be sailing your raft. If you are going to sail it on a river or in the sea, the raft needs to be quite large and more robust than if you are using a puddle or a bowl of water indoors. Rafts can be made from sticks tied together with string or glued (a hot glue gun is most effective). Make a mast from another twig, and a sail from a large leaf. For still water, a large leaf will serve as a base, with a smaller one for a sail.

Alternatively you can make rafts from craft sticks glued together, with a fabric sail, but this should be done only if the natural materials are too difficult to gather. If it is too complicated, a simple paper boat will float for a while, although it should be retrieved from the water before it sinks and becomes simply litter.

You can decorate your raft with flowers or make figures of people to sail it, but these should not be so heavy that they make the raft sink.

Feasting: burying the talents

You will need (per cake):
- One cupcake
- Gold and silver sugar balls or small chocolate coins
- Chocolate buttercream icing
- Two Oreo cookies with filling removed
- Green food colouring (optional)
- Fondant icing (optional)
- Knife for spreading
- Apple corer or cupcake corer
- Small plastic bag
- Rolling pin
- Paper plate

Crush the Oreo cookies by placing them in a plastic bag and hitting them gently with a rolling pin. (With younger children, you may need to do this preparation beforehand.)

Using the corer, remove the central core from the cupcake and put it to one side. If a corer is not available, carefully cut a small circle from the centre of the cupcake and set it aside, then dig out a hole from the centre of the cake.

Fill the hole with gold and silver balls or small chocolate coins.

Cover with chocolate buttercream icing and sprinkle with Oreo crumbs to look like soil. Alternatively, you could make a green field with buttercream icing and green food colouring, adding flowers made from fondant icing.

Celebrating: exploring water

Depending on your water source, any number of water-based activities can take place. If you are by the sea, try wave jumping: wait for a wave, then see if you can jump over it, as high as you can. If the group holds hands, you can try all jumping over the same wave at the same time.

If you have access to a small, shallow river or stream, try your hand at dam building. Select a spot where the river flows between some large stones or around a rock or log—a place where a small side stream has been created. Using large stones or sticks, begin to build a wall in the sidestream. Fill in any gaps with smaller stones, and build above the water line with stones, mud or sticks.

Notice how the water constantly changes direction, always trying to find a way through, running faster as the gaps become narrower. If you succeed in damming the sidestream completely, see the effect on the rest of the river— how the water builds up and spreads out. When your area of water has settled, try sailing your raft on it.

Make sure that, at the end of the activity, the dam is dismantled and the river resumes its original course.

Parts of ponds and puddles can also be dammed in the same way. Simply section off a small area of the water and try to prevent any more water spreading into it.

If you do not have access to natural water, you can experiment with dam building indoors, using a large, flat-bottomed container, such as a plastic drawer of the type used for underbed storage. Simply fill the container with sand and pack it down hard. Make the outline of a river in the sand, then construct your dam at a point along your projected river. You can use craft sticks, twigs, stones, matchsticks and so on.

When you think the dam will hold, slowly pour in water from one end of the river course. If the dam starts to collapse, work to block up all the holes before it falls down. When your dam is secure, you can widen the upstream area to make a lake for sailing your rafts.

Light

One day Jesus walked up the hillside overlooking Lake Galilee. He sat down and began to talk to the people about the way God wanted them to live their lives.

'The people who are happy are not the proud ones who think highly of themselves, but those who know how much they need God's help and forgiveness,' Jesus said. 'If you follow God's ways, you will be like a little salt in the cooking pot, making the whole meal taste good; or like a lamp shining brightly in a dark place, bringing light so that all can see.'

BARNABAS CHILDREN'S BIBLE, NO. 262 (MATTHEW 5:3, 13–15)

Reflecting on the story

It is always surprising to learn that the most stressful jobs and situations are often not those held by heads of large corporations or institutions, but those held by people who work in the lowliest positions. A chief executive may suffer less from stress than the person who cleans his office, for example, or the manager of a coffee shop may feel less pressure than the apprentice coffee maker. This is because stress is often associated with a feeling of powerlessness, of being unable to impact one's surroundings or affect one's future. This sense of helplessness is also suffered by children, who spend much time being told where to go and when, and what to do and how to do it when they get there.

This simple assertion recorded by Matthew can do much to restore our confidence in our ability to make a difference, our belief that what we say and do does matter. 'You are the light of the world,' says Christ, and he does not add any qualifying statements or introduce any conditions. We will not become lights if we behave in a certain way: we already have that status through God's grace and love. We are reminded that everything we do and say is important and has significance, not just in the eyes of our creator who made us or Jesus who died for us, but for the people who share our lives and witness our actions.

Even the smallest gesture of loving kindness to a friend, neighbour or stranger spreads the light of Christ's love further into the world, so every single one of us can become part of Christ's redeeming action in a fearful world, where darkness is prevalent. The more we act out our commission as light in the world, the more confidence we will gain in our role and the more love will be shared with those who need it.

Activities

Preparation

This session explores light in all its forms. Obviously, a sunny day is more useful than one that is overcast or rainy, but even the gloomiest summer days are long and light-filled. Once again, a large open space is a good place to begin, but more interest will be gained if your site is in a woodland or area containing large trees and bushes. As with all activities concerned with sunlight, it is important to emphasise that people should never look at the sun with the naked eye. If you are inside, some flexible light sources, such as torches or side lights, will be useful.

Being, looking, listening

Take some time to look at the effect of the sunlight on your surroundings. Experiment with the many different ways you can see this effect. Lie down beneath a tree and look up at the sky, noticing the way the sunlight is refracted and reflected by the leaves, and the way they scatter the light in all directions. Look at a patch of bare earth or lawn and see the shadows caused by clouds across the sun. Notice how the surfaces of pools, streams and rivers seem almost alive when the sun catches the water droplets, making them sparkle and dance.

Stand with your back to the sun and look at your shadow, how it grows smaller or larger depending on where the sun is. Try to make up a shadow dance with a partner, so that your shadows touch but your actual bodies remain at a distance from each other. Explore the shadows made by different objects: make puppets using twigs and leaves to fool the eye into thinking that objects are not what they seem. Try to make a shadow circle with your group, or a large pattern on the ground.

Use scraps of glass or shiny objects, such as foil or tin cans or the glass of your watch, to make pinpoints of light dance on the ground and in the air. Make them chase each other until the clouds cover the sun and they disappear.

Collecting: translucent objects

Search for natural objects that are translucent—flower petals, thin leaves and grasses are all good. Try to find a wide selection of sizes and colours, without making them too large for the craft. If you are by a river or at the seashore, look for pieces of coloured glass that have been rubbed smooth by the water.

Creating: a creation window

You will need (per window):

- Two paper plates
- Scissors
- Clear sticky-backed plastic
- Glue
- A hole punch
- Length of wool or string

Cut the central circles from the paper plates, so that you are left with the rims. Cut two pieces of sticky-backed plastic that are just smaller than the diameter of the outer circle of the plate, and larger than the hole in the middle. This stage may be best done in advance of your Outdoor Church gathering.

Make a pattern on one of the pieces of sticky-backed plastic (having first peeled off the backing) using the natural objects you have collected, being careful to keep within the borders of the central space.

Seal your picture with the other piece of plastic, then glue it between the two paper plates.

Punch a hole near the edge of the plate and thread some wool through it for hanging. Display your picture in a place where it can catch the light.

Feasting: candles

You will need (per candle):
- One jam sandwich biscuit
- One digestive biscuit
- 1 tbsp buttercream icing
- Half a banana
- A short length of licorice shoelace
- A short length of red sweet shoelace
- One mini marshmallow
- Knives for spreading and cutting
- Cocktail sticks
- Paper plate

Attach the jam sandwich biscuit to the digestive biscuit with buttercream icing. Peel the banana and cut a 5-centimetre length with a straight top and bottom.

Using a cocktail stick to make a pilot hole, push a small length of licorice lace into one end of the banana as a wick.

Attach the banana candle to the biscuit base with buttercream icing.

Loop a small piece of red lace and put both ends into the top of the mini marshmallow to make a fingergrip for your candlestick. Fasten this to the digestive biscuit at one edge with icing. (If crafting with younger children, it might be easier to miss out this step.)

NB: don't peel the bananas too long in advance or they will turn brown. The browning process can be slowed by painting the peeled banana with lemon juice or with a vitamin C tablet dissolved in water, but it is still best to make and eat the craft in one sitting.

Celebrating: shadow puppets and soap bubbles

Many of the looking and listening activities can be undertaken in a group: the task of making large shadow puppets using natural materials is particularly appropriate for group work. The most important thing is to find a position where the sunlight casts the best shadow. Choose simple shapes and use string or long grass to attach objects to each other to create people and animals.

Alternatively, explore the effect of light upon soap bubbles, using either small tubs of bubble mixture (which can be bought very cheaply) or giant soap bubbles:

You will need:
- 1 litre water
- 150 ml washing-up liquid
- 30 ml glycerine

Stir all the ingredients gently until they are mixed, then leave, preferably overnight. You may have to experiment with the proportions of each liquid, depending on the type you use. It is best to do this in advance, although you can make the investigation part of the activity.

Make giant bubble wands using metal coathangers. These can be bent into squares and diamonds as well as circles.

Watch how the bubbles catch the light, and the different colours that move within them. Notice how they float and turn in the breeze, and how objects change shape if you look at them through the bubbles.

It is best if you make your soap bubbles outside, preferably on grass. Soap bubble mixture is incredibly slippery, and, if you are inside, your floor will rapidly be in danger of becoming like an ice rink as soap bubbles explode over it.

Leaven

He told them another parable: 'The kingdom of heaven is like yeast that a woman took and mixed in with three measures of flour until all of it was leavened.'

MATTHEW 13:33

Reflecting on the story

During an assembly at our local primary school, I asked the children what they thought heaven was like. For the most part, they had fairly standard answers: it was up in the clouds, there was a lot of white everywhere, it was pretty good, and so on. Then I asked them to consider the qualities of the 'kingdom of heaven', linking it with the phrase in the Lord's prayer, 'Your kingdom come'. This produced more thoughtful and personal answers. It was less of a place somewhere distant in time and space, and more of an attitude, the children decided. It concerned people and relationships, and, more importantly, they could play a part within in, working to bring it closer. We spent time discussing what actions might bring this about. There was an interesting difference between an impersonal construct (heaven) and something with real potential that even children could affect and influence.

In many ways, Jesus' parables about the kingdom of heaven seek to do the same thing—to bring the kingdom of heaven within the reach of our understanding, and to remind us that we all have a role in playing it out. In particular, the story of the woman making bread and adding leaven, or yeast, shows how our actions, small and insignificant though they might appear to us and to those around us, can play a vital part in the salvation of our world. Like the action of that small amount of yeast among mounds of flour, God's kingdom may not always be highly visible but it is always there. It may not appear to be very much, but then, it doesn't take much. Most importantly of all, every single one of us has within us the potential to change the world, however slightly, edging the kingdom ever closer.

Activities

Preparation

The parable of the leaven gives us the opportunity to look at the many wonderful things to eat that grow in the wild. This is an exciting adventure but also one fraught with hazard. Great care must be taken to emphasise the importance of being quite sure of what we eat, and never randomly picking berries from trees. Plenty of adults should be present to monitor the food gathering. If you have worries about safety, you can always bring food outside and share a simple picnic. Even the most everyday food tastes different when eaten outdoors.

Being, looking, listening

The parable of the yeast in the bread dough reminds us of the importance of little things. For this session, some patience will be required, and very small people may need to be given a second, more active option if their concentration has a short timespan.

Find a space that is large enough to sit or lie on. If the ground is damp, you may want to think about bringing dustbin sacks or plastic sheeting. Then simply be still and look around carefully until you spot an insect. Examine it carefully without touching or disturbing it in any way. Look at its shape, the way its legs work, and think about whether it has any protection from predators. Watch the way it moves, and try to trace the pattern of its movements. Think of words that might describe how the insect looks, and more words for the way it moves.

Keep your eyes on the same insect for as long as possible, patiently observing where it goes and what it does. Is it collecting food? Does it move fast or slowly? Is it on its own or with other similar insects? Where do you imagine it comes from and where might it be going? Focus all your attention on this one tiny insect, easily ignored, a very small part of God's great universe.

Collecting: wild food

Gather food for an outdoor feast. As well as the common things such as blackberries, look for other foods. Lime flowers, which appear in July, make a delicious tea. Rose petals and clover flowers can be gathered for crystallising, and the tops of stinging nettles, picked with gloves on, make a wonderful soup. Err on the side of caution, however, unless you have a wild-food expert with you: better not to pick it if you have any doubts at all.

Creating: printing

Make print-pictures with vegetables. Gather a collection of vegetables that have clear prints when halved, such as peppers, mushrooms, aubergines, broccoli and cauliflower. You can use vegetables such as potatoes and swedes if you want to carve shapes out of them, but it might be better simply to use the shapes of the vegetables themselves to make patterns.

Pour paint into shallow trays, then make prints on paper with your vegetables. You might need to experiment with the consistency of paint so that it neither drips off nor fails to cover the vegetable. You can use fabric paint to decorate place mats, tea towels and aprons, or you can print on to card and laminate the results to make a place mat.

Feasting: soda bread

The obvious craft for this parable is, of course, bread-making. Ideally, you should have several batches of ordinary dough prepared beforehand, so that all the children need to do is knead their batch of dough and make bread rolls in whatever shape they like. However, the rolls will still require a second proving and not many churches boast a warm enough place for this. The timing of the activity can also be a challenge, as there will need to be quite a long interval for proving, then baking.

An alternative is to make soda bread, which needs no kneading or proving, and only takes 15 minutes to bake. It also has the advantage that the dough does not need to be prepared in advance but can be made as part of the activity. Buttermilk is now available in most large supermarkets; it can be found sometimes with the cream, sometimes with the milk, and occasionally with the yoghurt.

You will need:
- 320 g self-raising flour
- ½ tsp salt
- 1 tsp bicarbonate of soda
- 300 ml buttermilk
- Mixing bowl and spoon
- Knives for mixing
- Floured board

These quantities make about twelve rolls, depending on size.

Mix all the dry ingredients together in a bowl. Make a well in the centre and pour in the buttermilk. Mix with a knife until the mixture starts to come together. Tip out on to a floured board and knead lightly until a ball of dough is formed.

Shape the dough into rolls, then cook at 180°C/Gas Mark 4 for about ten minutes.

Celebrating: eating outside

Have an outdoor feast, using all the food that you have gathered and also your freshly baked bread rolls. Make nettle soup using the recipe that follows. If you can, keep it warm over a fire, or in a thermos flask if a fire is not available.

You will need (for four servings):

- One carrot
- One potato
- One onion
- Cooking oil
- 1 litre of vegetable stock
- 400 g nettle leaves
- 1 tbsp double cream (optional)

Peel the carrot, potato and onion and chop them into small cubes. Soften them by heating them in cooking oil for about ten minutes. Add the vegetable stock and simmer for a further ten minutes. When the vegetables are soft, add the nettle leaves (pick small young leaves from the tips of the nettle plant). Simmer for one minute, then blend. You can stir in a tablespoon of double cream before serving if you like.

If finding wild food has been too challenging, display your bread and other simple foodstuffs, such as cheese and seasonal fruit, in bowls lined with leaves. Be prepared to eat with your fingers.

Summer celebration: Pentecost

Jerusalem was full of visitors from all over the world. They had come for the festival of Pentecost.

The believers were together in one room when, suddenly, a sound like a strong wind blew through the house, filling it with noise. Something like flames seemed to burn in the air and touch each person there. As the Holy Spirit touched them, they all began to speak in other languages.

The noise from the house attracted a crowd.

'What's happening?' some of them said. 'I can understand what these men are saying. They are speaking in my language, talking about God. How is this possible?'

'They're drunk!' laughed others.

'No, we're not!' said Peter, coming out to speak to the crowd. 'It's only nine o'clock in the morning.' Then Peter stood up to teach all those who would listen…

That day 3000 people became followers of Jesus.

BARNABAS CHILDREN'S BIBLE, NO. 319 (ACTS 2:1–15, 41)

Reflecting on the story

It is almost a cliché, nowadays: we say that Pentecost is 'the birthday of the church', and we celebrate it perhaps by inflating balloons with helium and watching them float into the sky, or lighting candles and making crowns with red tissue paper to indicate the Holy Spirit. Often, we are so concerned with the external effect—balloons, flames and a huge birthday cake for the whole church, for example—that the truly astonishing nature of the event that happened in a small, scruffy room in the narrow streets of Jerusalem may pass us by.

It was a fragile event, that first Pentecost—a gift of extraordinary, life-transforming power bestowed on the most unlikely group of men and women. After all, these were the people who had abandoned their beloved leader and left him to die. These were the people who, far from proclaiming a new era, had shut themselves away for fear of reprisals from the old authorities.

A mixed bag of flawed, failing human beings they were, but that did not matter. In one moment, all that changed, and those first disciples became the instruments of God through the Holy Spirit, and thus they were capable of all things. After the fire and the wind had touched them and entered them, they started to do things they had never done before. Fear was overcome by the burning need to share the news of Christ with everyone they met. Their hesitation to speak out loud and live up to the challenges that Jesus had placed before them—loving one another, forgiving one another, healing one another—was replaced by an energy and enthusiasm to make all people brothers and sisters in love.

Pentecost is indeed the birthday of the church, a corporate affair, but it is also the opportunity for rebirth for all of us as we celebrate God's gift of the Holy Spirit to us all, individually and as a loving community.

Activities

Preparation

Energies and attention for this session will be directed towards preparing for a huge outdoor celebration. We will be collecting the raw materials for musical instruments and decorations for an outdoor arena, which everyone can join together to construct. A suitable site for the group gathering should be scouted beforehand, or, if the decision is made to hold the celebration in a church building, arrangements will need to be made for its decoration. Additional raw materials might be needed, such as flowers and seeds, as well as extra musical instruments to supplement the woodland orchestra.

Being, looking, listening

You will need a selection of scarves or other items to serve as blindfolds.

This activity requires people to work together in groups of two or three. If children are working together, care should be taken that they are old enough to undertake the activity responsibly. A mixed-age group is preferred, especially as children will enjoy the unusual feeling of being responsible for the safety of an older person and leading them around.

Once you have established your pairs or small groups, invite one person in each group to wear a blindfold. The other members of the group must lead them round carefully, inviting them to listen to the sounds of the area they are in. It is a good idea for the other group members to be as quiet as possible so that those who are wearing the blindfolds can hear sounds beyond people's chatter. Walk slowly, paying attention to the path of those who cannot see. Lead them to areas with interesting textures underfoot, and give them various objects to hold or smell, encouraging them to describe them using the senses that remain after sight has been removed.

Take it in turns to wear the blindfold, then encourage the group members to share their reflections on their experience.

Collecting: material for a celebration

Gather objects to make decorations and musical instruments for the Pentecost celebration. Remind the group not to pick anything that is poisonous or to gather material in such a way that the plant or the environment is damaged. Be creative about the things you choose; even small flowers, such as daisies, can be linked together to make chains.

Look for seeds or small stones to make shakers, as well as pine cones, sturdy sticks and dead leaves—anything that will make an interesting sound.

Creating: musical instruments and party decorations

Arrange flowers in small groups or link them together to make garlands for decorations. Mix flowers and leaves, dead things and living things all together. Do not be bound by the traditional rules of decorations or arrangements.

Make natural musical instruments. Pine cones can be scraped with sticks to make a staccato sound, sticks make natural wood blocks, and seeds can be placed inside empty yoghurt pots or small plastic tubs to make shakers, which can be decorated with acrylic paint or stickers. Scrunch up dead leaves for a dry, rustling percussion sound. Fill an empty cardboard box with seeds, then use a stick to beat it to make a rattling drum.

Feasting: Pentecost flames

You will need (per flame):
- One flat-bottomed ice cream cone
- One cupcake of a size to fit inside the cone at the top
- Buttercream icing, coloured yellow
- One strawberry ribbon sweet or Fruit Winder
- Scissors
- Knife
- Icing bag and nozzle, or plastic food bag
- Paper plate

Flat-bottomed ice cream cones can be found at major supermarkets. For small cupcakes, you can always make them slightly larger and trim them down.

If you have a large group, it is possible to manage without proper icing bags. Simply cut the corner from a plastic food bag to make your own.

If you are working with small children, cut the shape of a flame from the strawberry ribbon sweets and fill the icing bags with buttercream icing beforehand.

Unwrap the cupcake from its paper case and fit it inside the ice cream cone so that the top of the cake is more or less level with the top of the cone.

Fill the icing bag with yellow buttercream icing and pipe rosettes (or blobs) over the top of the cupcake so that it is completely covered. Very small children may find this too technically stretching: spreading with a knife is fine.

Cut a flame shape from the strawberry ribbon or Fruit Winder and place it in the middle of the icing.

Celebrating: outdoor concert space

Create and decorate an outside celebration space. Depending on how ambitious you are and how flexible your space is, push large sticks into the ground to form the boundary of the area, then weave flexible sticks and branches in between them to form a woven fence. If the space does not permit this, place tall sticks in the ground at intervals and decorate with garlands of flowers, leaves and interesting natural objects.

If the group is older, make a stage area, with a backdrop of sticks and branches decorated with flowers and leaves. You might want to build an altar from logs or stones, or a focal area in the centre of your space.

If you are inside a building, bring as much of the outdoors in as possible. Build a focal point using natural objects, and arrange branches, leaves and flowers around your worship space. Make garlands using paper flowers threaded on to string if you do not have access to real ones.

Celebrate Pentecost with songs and dance, using your musical instruments.

AUTUMN

Autumn can be a very mixed season. The weather can be absolutely glorious, with long golden days bringing the opportunity to revel in the riot of colours that can be found on trees and bushes, as green turns to yellows, oranges and browns. We observe the bustling activity of woodland animals gathering as much food as possible against the approaching winter. It can be a time for us to gather, too—picking blackberries and eating them straight from the bush, collecting conkers to make animals or challenge others to battle, and making wonderful collages of leaves and feathers. However, autumn can also bring mist and rain, with long grey days that are damp and cold. The gifts of nature can seem hidden then, as seeds fall to the ground and are buried beneath the debris of an ageing year. It is hard, at such times, to believe that anything will ever come of them, much less that in six months or so, green shoots will emerge from the darkness once again.

The sessions in this section look at prayer and its importance in the life of the church. Prayer is conversation with God, which involves listening as well as speaking. Answered prayers are wonderful things in which all can rejoice; they affirm our faith and deepen our trust. However, not all prayers are answered in a way that we like or even recognise, and these occasions offer a challenge to us, which should be met head on and brought back to God. Sometimes we have to be quiet and still to hear God's voice; sometimes it seems as if we do not hear it at all, so great is the sound of our busyness, our pain or our anger. Then we must trust that, in the depths of our souls, green shoots, still unperceived, are unfurling.

The friend at night

And [Jesus] said to [his disciples], 'Suppose one of you has a friend, and you go to him at midnight and say to him, "Friend, lend me three loaves of bread; for a friend of mine has arrived, and I have nothing to set before him." And he answers from within, "Do not bother me; the door has already been locked, and my children are with me in bed; I cannot get up and give you anything." I tell you, even though he will not get up and give him anything because he is his friend, at least because of his persistence he will get up and give him whatever he needs.

'So I say to you, Ask, and it will be given to you; search, and you will find; knock, and the door will be opened for you. For everyone who asks receives, and everyone who searches finds, and for everyone who knocks, the door will be opened.'

LUKE 11:5–10

Reflecting on the story

Sometimes it can seem as if we pray and pray and still nothing happens, as if we spend our time asking and waiting and hoping but there is no answer. Jesus' response to this is found here in Luke, where our prayers are compared to the request of a friend for some food. We are invited to take the part both of the man who is asking for the food and the person who has been disturbed in his sleep by the demands of his friend. Who would not, in need, persist in asking for what was necessary? The man has an unexpected guest and it is important for the rules of hospitality to be observed; his guest must be fed. If a negative answer is received, the man must continue to ask, for he knows that what he asks is both needful and right.

So too must we be persistent in asking, but also convinced that what we request is indeed a good and necessary thing. The sleeper, however disrupted his night has become, must in his turn respond to the request because it complies with the rules of friendship and community. Thus will God respond in the light of the covenant of love that he has made with all of us.

Jesus reminds us that if we do but ask, all the gifts of heaven are waiting for us. Seeking God, searching for evidence of his love and travelling deeper into a relationship with him are lifelong activities. They can seem difficult and fruitless at times, but persistence will always bring rewards. In the famous picture by Holman Hunt, *The Light of the World*, Christ is shown standing outside a doorway, his hand raised to knock. There is no handle on his side: the message is that Jesus is always there for us, but it is we ourselves who have to open the door to him.

ACTIVITIES

PREPARATION

The theme for this session is that of seeking and looking. We are encouraged to look in unexpected places, and to look again at familiar sights, this time examining them more closely. Some treasures can be found only by picking up clues, such as the sound of movements; others, like the potential of seeds and bulbs, are covered and closed. As we play hide-and-seek, we too become that which is sought, just as Jesus reaches out to all of us, to lead us out of darkness into the light of his love.

BEING, LOOKING, LISTENING

Go on a 'sound safari'. Walking as quietly as you can, listen carefully for the different sounds that are all around you. Listen particularly for the rustling of branches and leaves that indicates the presence of small animals or birds. Listen for the obvious sounds, such as birdsong and dogs barking, but listen carefully too for the quieter, less obtrusive noises of smaller birds and animals, and even insects. Stop frequently, standing as still as you can so that animals that may have been startled by your movements have a chance to settle down again and recover their nerve. If you hear movements, stay still; creatures may continue to make interesting sounds or, even better, you may spot the animals themselves.

Don't be afraid to crouch down by a large patch of undergrowth or near some long grass. If you are very quiet, you may even hear the rustling and clicking of beetles and other large insects.

If you have a mobile phone with a microphone, you might be able to record these sounds and share them with others. Or you could make patterns that are suggested to you by the sounds of the animals you have heard: try spikey triangles for sharp noises, or smoother curves for more gentle ones. What sort of patterns do rustles and creaks look like?

Collecting: seeds

Autumn is a time when flowers and trees begin to drop seeds and fruit, with a view to next year's young plants. Go on a seed hunt, carefully gathering as many different seeds as possible. Some seeds will be easy to collect, such as poppy, which can be gathered by gently shaking the seed heads. Others will require more skill. Take care that you do not damage the growing plant while you are gathering, and do not take all the seeds from one plant or area. Don't forget that things such as conkers and acorns are seeds too.

Creating: seed collage

Make a picture using the seeds you have gathered. You could make anything you like, or perhaps you could choose to depict the flower that will grow from the seeds you are using. If you have not gathered enough seeds, you can supplement them with shop-bought ones such as sunflower, poppy, corn or wheat. If you are indoors, you can make your collage in the traditional way, on paper with a strong glue, such as washable PVA. If you are outside, think of different backgrounds for your collage—perhaps some large leaves or a smooth piece of bark.

Feasting: a front door

You will need (for one door):
- One rectangular slice of cake
- Chocolate buttercream icing
- A small amount of red fondant icing
- One rectangular plain biscuit

- One rectangular ice cream wafer
- Knife for spreading
- Heart-shaped cookie cutter, small enough to fit on biscuit
- Rolling pin
- Board for rolling
- Baking paper
- Pencil
- Scissors
- Paper plate
- Writing icing (optional)
- Sugar flowers (optional)

Your slice of cake will need to be quite thick if you want your door to stand upright—a good two or three centimetres. For younger children, you might want to cut out small hearts from the fondant icing in advance, as well as the door shape from the wafer.

Lay the slice of cake flat on a paper plate and spread it with chocolate buttercream icing. Roll out the red fondant icing and cut out a small heart shape.

Carefully trace the shape of the plain biscuit on to the baking paper and cut out the shape. Using the baking paper as a guide, cut out a rectangle from the ice cream wafer with a knife or scissors. You may need a few attempts to get this right. If it is too difficult, simply cut three lengths of wafer for the sides and top of the door frame separately.

Place the door-frame wafer carefully on to the iced cake slice. Place the fondant heart in the space inside the door frame. Now stand the cake up.

Carefully fit the biscuit door into the door frame. If you like, you can position the biscuit so that it looks as if the door is slightly open, but this is quite tricky; otherwise, simply place it flat over the fondant heart.

Older children may want to decorate the door with writing icing and put sugar flowers around the bottom of the door.

Celebrating: hunting and seeking

Play hide-and-seek games. Traditional hide-and-seek is good if there are lots of places to hide; as an alternative, you may want to play sardines, where one person hides and anyone who finds them hides with them until only one person is left looking. If there are few places to hide, play 'back to base', where one person has to 'tag' the others before they can reach the designated base. Various handicaps can be imposed to make the games fair for all-age groups, but the rules must be carefully spelt out and agreed on before the game commences, to avoid arguments.

If you don't want to play hide-and-seek with people, try the same game with objects—the size depending on the age and skill of your group. Hide clean tin cans or brightly coloured cloths, with the winner being the person or team that finds the most objects.

The faithful servant

'Be dressed for action and have your lamps lit; be like those who are waiting for their master to return from the wedding banquet, so that they may open the door for him as soon as he comes and knocks. Blessed are those slaves whom the master finds alert when he comes; truly I tell you, he will fasten his belt and have them sit down to eat, and he will come and serve them. If he comes during the middle of the night, or near dawn, and finds them so, blessed are those slaves.'

LUKE 12:35–88

Reflecting on the story

There is a real feeling of urgency in this passage, as Jesus tells his followers that they must be prepared at all times for the coming of the kingdom. This exhortation is spoken just after Jesus has assured everyone of God's loving kindness and provision for them in all matters. They need not worry about what to eat or drink or wear; instead, they are to focus on the more important matters. The followers of Christ must seek to build up treasure in heaven, not on earth, for that is their ultimate destination.

In the meantime, we must be alert for the signs of the coming kingdom, for we do not know when it will arrive. We live in the waiting times, in the time of preparation, but this is not an excuse for sleepiness or inactivity. Just as the good slaves keep watch throughout the darkest times of the night, so we too, during the darkest times of our lives, must not give up hope or cease to pray. Notice that the master finally arrives near dawn, when the endurance and energy of human beings is at its lowest. How grateful must the slaves have been when they finally heard the master approach! How relieved that they could soon eat and rest, secure in the knowledge that their job had been carried out faithfully! And their reward is greater than this, for the master invites them to eat at his table and even goes so far as to serve them himself.

Surely the promise of God's imminent arrival, and the prospect of sharing in his kingdom with him, is enough to keep us watching and waiting, alert for the signs of his approach, ready to rejoice at his arrival.

Activities

Preparation

We are continuing the theme of looking and listening, viewing the landscape from unusual angles, focusing on things above our heads and beneath our feet. The signs of the kingdom are here, but often they are hidden, just as some of the most beautiful natural objects are not always in plain view but have to be carefully sought.

Being, looking, listening

Go on an 'up and down' walk. Spend half your time looking up into the air, and the other half looking closely at the ground. Look especially at the flight of any birds you see. Watch out for birds flying south for warmer climates, and notice the shapes they make. Look at the way different birds fly, whether rapidly with beating wings, or more slowly, taking advantage of the air currents to soar up and glide down. Try to follow the entire flight of a bird, from taking off from a tree to landing again somewhere else.

When your neck aches with looking up, walk along looking at the ground, searching for any evidence that animals have passed by. Look for animal tracks or droppings, and places where branches have been bent back or the grass worn away by animal feet. Look at the edges of streams and puddles for evidence of bird life—footprints in the mud, or bird droppings. If you find any animals, follow them with your eyes as far as you can; see how they move and where they go. Look for signs of animal or insect homes—small holes dug in the sides of soft earth banks, hollowed-out places in tree trunks or among roots, large busy ant nests or tiny, unobtrusive shelters for beetles and woodlice.

Collecting: leaves

Collection is focused once more on things above our heads and below our feet. Collect as many different types of leaf as possible. For the 'Creating' project, fleshy leaves will be better, such as magnolia, hydrangea or rhododendron. Make sure they are fresh and green rather than turning yellow or brown.

CREATING: LEAF SKELETONS

Create a large collage in the shape of an eye or a burning lamp. If you are using leaves, an eye pattern is very effective as it is mirrored by the shape of the leaves themselves. An extra dimension is added to this project if you create the collage using leaf skeletons.

Mix 20 g washing soda (sodium carbonate) with half a litre of water and bring to the boil. Add the leaves and simmer gently for 30 minutes. The leaves and the solution will turn a horrible brown colour but that is nothing to worry about.

Remove the leaves and, with a paintbrush or an old toothbrush, gently brush away the flesh, revealing the skeleton of the leaf. **IMPORTANT:** wear latex gloves for this, as washing soda is caustic.

If you want white leaf skeletons, soak them in a solution of bleach, taking care once again to wear protective gloves and clothing.

The skeletons can be coloured by placing them in a bowl of water with liquid food dye.

FEASTING: HOLDING A MINIATURE PARTY

What you use depends on what sort of meal you decide to make in miniature. The suggestions below are for a tea party, as, in my experience, this is the easiest option.

You will need:
- Slices of bread
- Margarine and sandwich fillings

- Plain fruit or sponge cake (or both)
- Small versions of biscuits, such as mini Oreo cookies, jam sandwich biscuits and so on
- Knives for spreading and cutting
- Very small cookie cutters in interesting shapes

For convenience, a dolls' tea set can be used. If you want to extend the length of the activity, cut out small plate shapes from card, which can be decorated as tea plates. They can be laminated later to increase their durability.

The crafting of the tea plates can be a separate activity, or you can download patterns from the internet and create your own laminated plates beforehand.

Make miniature sandwiches, cakes and so on, for a tea party. Cut the crusts off the bread slices or use cookie cutters to make tiny sandwiches in different shapes. Do the same with the cake slices. Leftover cake can be mixed with buttercream icing and moulded to make other cake or food shapes.

Arrange the food attractively on the plates, ready for your party.

Celebrating: a bird and animal hide

Make a hide from which you can watch birds and animals. If you have access to woodland, this is the easiest environment to use. It is easiest to build a den using a location that is already sheltered—between rocks, among fallen logs, under large bushes and shrubs. If the ground is damp, you may want to bring an old tarpaulin or plastic sheeting. If you think there might be a shortage of raw materials, sheeting can be used to provide the basic structure for your den as well.

Find old sticks and logs to build the frame of the hide, then fill in the gaps with leafy branches or more sticks. (Be aware that bracken is not recommended as it can house ticks which can be passed on to human beings.) Don't remove living branches from trees or bushes: you must respect the environment within which you are working. Make sure that you have an entrance way: if you like, you can build a structure to use as a door.

If your outdoor space lacks natural materials, bring a supply of sheeting, old tablecloths, some strong garden canes or stakes and string or pegs. Encourage the group to work together to build a large den or, if you need an easier project, invite smaller groups to make some that will shelter two or three people.

If there is no access to den-making materials for human beings, why not make a miniature den for dolls and teddy bears, or for imaginary small people or animals? This can be as fanciful as you like, using stones and twigs, leaves and cones. Bring string and pegs and, if the area is really sparse, junk modelling materials. Remember to remove it from the area at the end of the activity, however.

The Pharisee and the tax collector

He also told this parable to some who trusted in themselves that they were righteous and regarded others with contempt: 'Two men went up to the temple to pray, one a Pharisee and the other a tax-collector. The Pharisee, standing by himself, was praying thus, "God, I thank you that I am not like other people: thieves, rogues, adulterers, or even like this tax-collector. I fast twice a week; I give a tenth of all my income." But the tax-collector, standing far off, would not even look up to heaven, but was beating his breast and saying, "God, be merciful to me, a sinner!" I tell you, this man went down to his home justified rather than the other; for all who exalt themselves will be humbled, but all who humble themselves will be exalted.'

LUKE 18:9–14

Reflecting on the story

This parable is another challenge to us not to be so sure of ourselves and our innate righteousness that we start to imagine we are without sin. The Pharisee does all the right things in accordance with the law, but in his heart he is proud and arrogant. He scorns other people in his community and, when he compares himself to them, it appears to him that he is easily superior. So convinced is he that he is better than others he sees around him, he fails to realise how wrong his pride is, and how unprepared he is to admit his shortcomings. His attitude is not prayerful; he is not open to what God might be calling him to do, and he will not hear how he might change.

The tax collector, on the other hand, is aware that he has committed many errors and his way of life is not good, and he asks for God's mercy upon him. Admitting that we might be wrong is the first step along the path to change and growth. This parable reminds us also not to be fooled by the outside nature of a person, which might seem to be unappealing or wrong, but instead to try to look within and appreciate the goodness that is hidden there.

Activities

Preparation

The subject for this session is the horse chestnut tree and, in particular, its fruit, the conker. Prickly on the outside, it is ugly and harsh-looking when it falls from the tree in autumn, but break open that hard shell and a beautiful, shiny conker is revealed, its dark brown skin glowing against the white lining of the case—a hidden gift of nature.

Timing is quite important for this session. You need to find a horse chestnut tree that is just at the point where the conkers are falling to the ground. Horse chestnuts are common throughout England and very popular in parks, so, if you don't know where to find one, your nearest park is a good place to start. Once you have found your tree, it might be a good idea to gather some conkers in advance, just in case they have all been picked up when you get there. Collect them in their shells if you can.

For the 'Creating' activity, you might want to bring some cloves and star anise, and some knitting needles.

Being, Looking, Listening

Stand as close as possible to the trunk of a horse chestnut tree and spend some time looking at its bark. Feel its roughness under your hand. Look upwards into the branches of the tree: horse chestnut trees can grow as high as 36 metres. See how the leaves are arranged so that each one is in a slightly different place to the one above it, each in the best possible position to get the light it needs. Look at the colours of the leaves: chestnut trees are among the earliest to change colour in the autumn, and, by the time the conkers are falling, the leaves are many different shades of brown and orange. Notice the shape that is left on the twig where a leaf has dropped off: it looks like a horseshoe, complete with seven nails.

Pick up a conker, preferably one in its shell. Feel how rough the case is; see how spattered with brown spots and scattered with prickles it is. Carefully open up the case and contrast the outside with the smooth, creamy lining. See how the conker rests snugly in the case. Pop the conker out and hold it in your hand. Look up into the tree again and see how very many cases are hanging there among the branches, each containing a small, shining treasure like the one in your hand.

Collecting: CONKERS AND TWIGS

Gather a handful of conkers, with or without their shells. Look for small twigs with interesting shapes. These can be thin or thick, but try to make sure they are quite strong.

Creating: CONKER CREATURES

It is possible to make all sorts of models using conkers and their shells. Animals and people are the easiest. Conker cases make good hats, and flat conkers will enable the person or animal to stand up. Adults can assist by making holes with knitting needles so that twig limbs can be attached. If you have difficulty with twigs, matchsticks can be substituted, although they look a bit stark against the conker.

Cloves make good noses, and sections of star anise become fine ears. The more ambitious members of your group can make whole forest landscapes, using larger twigs inserted in big, flat conker bases as trees.

Feasting: CONKER TRUFFLES

You will need:
- 175 g melted chocolate
- 100 g crushed digestive biscuits
- 50 g softened butter
- 50 g icing sugar
- Melted green candy buttons
- Green sprinkles
- Mixing bowl and spoon
- Paper plate

The number of truffles you can get from these quantities depends on how big you make them, but they are quite rich so efforts should be made to keep them to a reasonable size.

Mix together the melted chocolate, biscuits, butter and icing sugar. Leave to cool for a while, then roll into small balls on a paper plate. Coat with melted green candy buttons (available from Hobbycraft or other craft shops), then roll in green sprinkles (from large supermarkets).

If the coating is too difficult, the truffles can simply be rolled in green sugar sprinkles. If your space does not have cooking facilities, the mixture can be made earlier and, if kept at room temperature, will remain mouldable.

Celebrating: games with leaves and conkers

If the day is dry, you might want to gather up piles of leaves and run and jump in them. See how many different sounds you can make using leaves—throwing them in the air, kicking them, crushing them beneath your feet and crunching them in your hands. Make up a story with sound effects made only from leaves: 'It was a cold and windy day, and the animals were running through the wood…'

Play conkers: make a hole in a conker and thread a string through it, of between 20 and 30 cm, tying a knot below the conker. One person holds the conker out to the side, well away from their body, while the other person has to use their conker to hit it. The winner is the one who hits the opponent's conker the most times, or even breaks it.

The widow and the judge

Then Jesus told his disciples a parable to show them that they should always pray and not give up. He said: 'In a certain town there was a judge who neither feared God nor cared what people thought. And there was a widow in that town who kept coming to him with the plea, "Grant me justice against my adversary."

'For some time he refused. But finally he said to himself, "Even though I don't fear God or care what people think, yet because this widow keeps bothering me, I will see that she gets justice, so that she won't eventually come and attack me!"'

And the Lord said, 'Listen to what the unjust judge says. And will not God bring about justice for his chosen ones, who cry out to him day and night? Will he keep putting them off? I tell you, he will see that they get justice, and quickly. However, when the Son of Man comes, will he find faith on the earth?'

LUKE 18:1–8 (NIV)

Reflecting on the story

Once again, Jesus is telling us a parable that will help us to learn about prayer, and, again, it can be interpreted in a number of different ways. As Luke tells us, it is intended to teach the disciples that they must be persistent in prayer, and we can liken the widow to ourselves, appealing day after day to the unjust judge to have mercy upon us until finally he breaks down and gives us what we want.

Of course, God is not unjust: Jesus is saying that the just and merciful God is bound to act more swiftly and kindly than the unjust judge. But we could look at the story from another angle. What if we see ourselves as unjust judges, who neither fear God nor care what people think? What if it is God who is continually pleading with us, crying out to us day and night, and who won't let us alone? What does God want from us that we are so reluctant to grant him? Perhaps, like the prodigal son, we have wandered far from our true home and need to be called back. Perhaps, like Jonah, God has a task for us that we are reluctant to take upon ourselves, fearing the amount of effort or courage it might need. Perhaps we have become so comfortable and set in our ways that we ignore a call to deeper commitment.

We may not always want to hear God's call, but, like the widow, God will continue, lovingly and persistently, until we turn to him with the words 'Your will, not mine, be done.'

Activities

Preparation

This time we are looking at the effect of the invisible wind on particular objects. Just as we cannot see our prayers but only the effects of them in our lives, so the wind itself cannot be seen, only the results of its actions. The crafts and activities for this session could also be used during the season of Pentecost, looking at the action of the Holy Spirit.

Being, looking, listening

Try to select a day when it is quite windy: one of those still, rainy autumn days will not produce such interesting effects. As you walk to the meeting place, notice how the wind is affecting the objects around you. Observe the patterns that the wind makes on any pools of water—ripples and even waves being blown about the surface. Listen to the sound the wind makes in the trees and shrubs. If you are walking through grassland, compare the sound of the wind on the grass with the noise of windblown leaves, especially those that have fallen to the ground. Notice how the currents of air blow objects such as leaves and other debris around, and observe the circular patterns of small eddies and flurries.

Stand still in your meeting place and feel the effect of the wind on your own self. Is the air dry or damp? Is it cold or slightly warm? How does the wind feel on your face or your hands? Can you tell what direction it is coming from? Lick your index finger and hold it up in the air. Does one side feel colder than the other because the wind is blowing from that direction and chilling your damp skin?

Collecting: things that will blow in the wind

Collect light, attractive objects to make a nature mobile. Things such as feathers, unusually shaped twigs, and leaves in interesting colours are all useful for this craft. Make sure you include two larger, sturdier sticks for the base of your mobile. You can also collect unusual items such as moss, shells or small stones.

If you are not making a mobile, wrap a piece of masking tape loosely around your wrist with the sticky side facing out. As you collect your objects, stick them on to the masking tape in patterns and shapes. By the end of your walk you will have a masking-tape nature bracelet.

Creating: a nature mobile

With some strong string, wrap together the two longer sticks you collected, to form a cross shape with equal arms. Leave one end of the string quite long so that you can hang the mobile up when it is finished. Then simply tie the other objects you gathered on to the mobile arms with lengths of string. Some of the objects, like sticks, will be easy to fasten. Others, like small stones, will need to be carefully attached if they are not to fall off in the wind.

If you make sure the strings are different lengths, you will get a more attractive effect at the end. However, if you want your mobile to make a noise as well as move in the wind, make some of the strings the same length and attach the larger objects so that they bump together in the breeze. You can use coloured wool or string if you want a brighter mobile.

Feasting: praying hands

You will need (per hand):
- Two thin slices of plain sponge cake (or bread)
- A selection of licorice string, strawberry laces and small jelly sweets
- Writing icing in different colours

- Jam for filling
- Knife for cutting
- Cookie cutter in the shape of a hand, or paper, pencil and scissors
- Paper

The sponge cake needs to be quite dense, such as a Madeira cake, and preferably a few days old. Younger children may need help with creating the shape of a hand in cake. As an alternative to a cookie cutter, you can get the children to draw round their own hand on paper and use this as a template.

Cut out the shape of a hand in both slices of cake, using either the cookie cutter or the paper template. Spread one slice with jam and place it on top of the other to form a sandwich. These are your praying hands.

Decorate the hands: use writing icing for 'nail varnish', make jewellery from licorice or strawberry laces and jelly sweets, or draw patterns with the writing icing.

Celebrating: fly a kite!

When it is windy enough, have a group kite-flying day. Small pocket kites can be purchased quite cheaply, or you can make them.

First, find two sticks, one about one-third longer than the other. The sticks need to be quite light, so that your kite flies easily: wooden barbeque skewers are a good start. Fasten them together firmly in a cross shape, with string or strong thread, tying about one third of the way along the longer stick, and in the middle of the shorter stick.

Draw a kite pattern—a diamond with two extended sides—on to a sturdy piece of paper or thin card and cut it out. The kite should be just a little larger than the sticks you have bound together. Either make a hole at each corner and thread string through the paper and round the sticks to fasten them together, or tape the sticks on to the paper using duct tape.

Measure another piece of string, just a little longer than the shorter stick, and tie it to each end of the stick. Tie a long piece of string from the middle of your pilot string. The long string will be the one you use for flying your kite. Attach ribbons or paper streamers to the corners of your kite for decoration.

Homemade kites are quite flimsy, so take plenty of spares for running repairs. Remember to keep kites away from roads and power lines, and never fly a kite in a storm.

Autumn celebration: Michaelmas

War broke out in heaven; Michael and his angels fought against the dragon. The dragon and his angels fought back, but they were defeated, and there was no longer any place for them in heaven. The great dragon was thrown down, that ancient serpent, who is called the Devil and Satan, the deceiver of the whole world—he was thrown down to the earth, and his angels were thrown down with him.

Then I heard a loud voice in heaven, proclaiming, 'Now have come the salvation and the power and the kingdom of our God and the authority of his Messiah, for the accuser of our comrades has been thrown down, who accuses them day and night before our God. But they have conquered him by the blood of the Lamb and by the word of their testimony, for they did not cling to life even in the face of death. Rejoice then, you heavens and those who dwell in them! But woe to the earth and the sea, for the devil has come down to you with great wrath, because he knows that his time is short!'

REVELATION 12:7–12

Reflecting on the story

The festival of Michaelmas, or St Michael and All Angels, has fallen out of favour with the church in recent years, although for centuries its significance within the secular calendar gave it a corresponding importance within the church. Michaelmas was one of the quarter days of the calendar, marking, in medieval times, the end of the husbandman's year. Crops were gathered in, and it was time to pay one's due to the landowner. Falling on 29 September, near the equinox, it is also associated with the beginning of autumn and days gradually getting shorter after the long sunlit hours of the summer. However, as our relationship with the land has become more tenuous, so too have our links with the quarter days and the rhythm of the seasons.

Celebrating Michaelmas is one way to remind ourselves of the changing patterns of our environment. For Christians, the feast is also a reminder that God reigns supreme over all of creation for all time. Satan has already been defeated, evil has been conquered and good has triumphed. The sufferings that remain to be endured by human beings while they live out their earthly existence are the last desperate efforts of Satan to cause as much damage as he can in the final skirmishes of a battle that has already been lost by the powers of darkness. We can be confident as we face the dark times of winter, either the season itself or our own personal winters, that God has the victory and evil has been banished. St Michael, the most powerful of all angels, is granted the soldier's wreath for his defence of heaven, while Satan and the rebellious angels languish on the perimeters of God's love, within his power still, but lost, by their own choice, to his love.

Activities

Preparation

Very often, Michaelmas focuses on the exciting drama of dragons or the ethereal beauty of angels. Outdoor Church presents different opportunities—the thrill and pleasure of building fires as a symbol of the light of God's love shining into the darkness as we approach the cold shadows of winter.

Being, looking, listening

For the 'Collecting' part of this session, you will be gathering firewood. Before you do so, it is essential to ensure that as few animals are disturbed by this process as possible. Find some large logs or tree trunks that have been cut from trees that were felled or died and toppled over, or some larger branches that have fallen off in storms. The bigger and older the logs and trunks, the better.

First, look closely at the parts of the logs that you can see easily. Notice the way that other plants have begun to grow over them as they age. Some logs will be covered with moss and lichen; others will be sprouting small green ferns. Still others will have begun to be covered with brambles and other low-growing plants. If the log is wet, look for mushrooms and algae. Carefully lift pieces of bark and moss to catch a glimpse of the creatures who have made their homes beneath them, taking care not to hurt the creatures themselves.

When you have done this, try to roll the log over or take a look beneath it. If it is too big to be moved, look at the places where the wood meets the ground. All sorts of creatures make their homes in dead and decaying wood, including woodlice, ants, many varieties of beetle and centipedes. Count how many different types you can see; observe the different ways in which they move and how fast they try to find a new place to shelter. When you have finished your observation, carefully replace the log where you found it.

Collecting: wood

In order to build a fire, you need firewood. If you are permitted to do so, gather wood in your meeting place. Remember that you will need a variety of sizes: small sticks are good for starting fires, while larger ones are needed to burn slowly and build up heat. If you are not allowed to gather wood, find some sturdy sticks, about 30 cm in length, for charcoal drawing.

Creating: charcoal drawing

If you do not have access to an open fire, you can buy charcoal sticks from an art supply shop, but it is more fun to make them. Wrap each stick carefully in aluminium foil, ensuring that the sticks are completely covered. Once the fire is well established and burning hot, place the stick bundles in the fire. After about 20 minutes they will have stopped flaming and smoke will no longer be coming from the bundle. Carefully remove them from the fire, using tongs or other implements, and wait until they have cooled before using them.

If you like, you can wrap leaves around one end of the charcoal sticks to make them easier and cleaner to hold.

Because charcoal is biodegradable and will wash away, you can have fun drawing on stones, fallen logs and bark as well as sturdy paper or card.

Feasting: tree cake

You will need (per cake):
- One cupcake
- 1 dsp chocolate buttercream icing
- One Flake bar
- A handful of yellow, green, brown and red Nerds sweets
- Black writing icing
- Crumbled Oreo cookies with filling removed (optional)
- Knife for spreading
- Paper plate

Spread the cupcake with the chocolate buttercream icing to look like soil. If you like, you can scatter it with Oreo crumbs, but this makes insect creation harder.

Breaking the Flake bar, carefully make the outline of a tree on the cake. It is better to do this horizontally rather than trying to get the tree to stand upright: branches are very challenging to make.

Use the yellow, green and brown Nerds as leaves for your branches. You can make insects from the red Nerds by piping legs and antennae (with black writing icing) on to one or two joined close together.

Alternatively, your Flake can be a fallen log, with Nerd insects crawling over and under it.

Celebrating: fire building and campfire cooking

If you are permitted to build a fire from scratch in your meeting place, this is the ideal scenario. Begin by clearing a patch of ground of any undergrowth that might catch light from sparks. In the centre of your clearing, dig a large shallow pit and surround it with stones or bricks to make a fireplace. This will contain the fire and also gives a clear safety boundary. Start building your fire with small twigs, then, as it begins to burn, gradually add larger sticks, followed by small logs.

When the fire has burned hot and red ashes are beginning to glow, this is the best time for campfire cooking. Wrap baking potatoes in foil and place them in the hot ashes to cook. Skewer thin sausages on sticks and hold them at the base of the flames to cook, turning your stick carefully and trying to prevent it from catching light in the flames. Make campfire bread rolls by combining flour and a pinch of salt with water to make a sticky dough, which can be wrapped round a stick in a sausage shape and toasted before being eaten with butter and jam.

If you have a limited amount of time, you might want to precook your food so that it only needs heating up on the fire, being careful to make sure it is properly hot before being eaten. Alternatively, toasted marshmallows are a very simple and quick campfire cookery experience.

If you are not able to build a fire, bring some portable foil barbecues to your space, making sure you take them away again.

NB: All activities relating to fire are inherently dangerous and great care should be taken that the fire is supervised at all times. Any children participating in the event should be kept at a safe distance from the fire pit. Cooking activities are great fun but children should be instructed first on how to cook safely and told to keep away from the fire unless they are in the company of an adult. Access to water, either in the form of a stream or pond, or in jerry cans placed nearby, should be ensured, and first-aid supplies kept close to hand.

WINTER

The first half of the winter season is, for children and adults alike, largely focused on preparations for Christmas. During the early winter months of November and December, excitement grows as thoughts turn towards that most popular celebration in the Christian calendar. All too often, the season of Epiphany and Candlemas coincides with a feeling of anticlimax and a dread of the continuing cold and dark, making the days seem longer even though the hours of daylight are shorter. Weary of being kept inside by bad weather, we long for the approach of spring, bringing with it brighter days filled with flowers and blossom. Birds and animals struggle to find enough food to see them through the famine times, and the harshness of the cold takes its toll on all living creatures. However, for the earth, this winter season is a vital time to pause and prepare before the hectic days of spring growth. The landscape, though silent, is not still. Beneath the ground, new seeds are waiting for the first warm days, the buds of trees are just beginning to develop and already signs of hope can be seen in the first hesitant snowdrops as they hang their bell-like blooms over the hard, frosty soil.

Outdoor Church focuses on waiting and stillness: we take silent walks and look for signs of spring, aware that this season, like the others, holds a beauty all its own. The parables focus on searching for lost objects, just as we look for signs of spring, but equally reflect on the importance of winter as a time during which the ground prepares to support future growth. The festival of light can be celebrated either at St Lucia, early in the season, or Candlemas, 40 days after the nativity, as we turn away from Christmas and look towards the cross.

The lost sheep

Many of the Pharisees and teachers of the law criticised Jesus because he spent time with ordinary people, many of whom they thought were sinners, doing things that were wrong.

'If you owned 100 sheep,' Jesus said to them, 'and one of them was lost, what would you do? Leave it to die and be content with the 99 that are safe in the sheep pen? No, you would go in search of the one that was lost. You would look everywhere until it was found, then you would be happier over that one lost sheep than all the others. So it is with God. He cares about all the sheep, and will not be happy till he has saved the one who has wandered away from the right path.'

BARNABAS CHILDREN'S BIBLE, NO. 281 (MATTHEW 18:12–13)

Reflecting on the story

Whenever I tell this story to young children (and I do so at least twice a year) I am always touched by the rapt attention of the youngest listener to the plight of the lost sheep. There is a universal fear being articulated within this story—that of not knowing where we are, of having strayed away from the person or group of people that constitutes our security and safety, to an unfamiliar place where we find ourselves alone. The panic and fear of the sheep are emotions that everyone has felt, even if only for a moment, reminding us of the time when, as a small child, suddenly the person caring for us was not to be seen and we were gripped by a feeling of abandonment.

Sadly, for many people, the feeling of being lost and alone is one that persists for many years, with a lonely upbringing developing into a lonely adulthood. Others may experience the loss of loved ones, which leads to a time of being alone, feeling lost and unloved. We, within our communities and churches, can do much to ameliorate this sense of separation, by acts of friendship and sharing, drawing others into a loving circle of kindness.

The relief of the sheep when the shepherd's patient searching results in their being reunited with each other brings huge smiles to the faces of the young listeners, as they hear how pleased both shepherd and sheep are that they can return together to their home. So, too, we will experience joy and relief when our own good shepherd comes looking for us in the dark, fearful places to which we have wandered. Then, all our loneliness and all our losses will be swept away in the warmth of God's love as he gathers us gently in his arms to lead us to our eternal home.

Activities

Preparation

Just as the lost sheep experiences what it is to be alone as well as life among the other sheep, so too, at different times of our lives, we experience both community and separation.

This session begins with a reflection on the experience of separateness, then draws people together to form a group artwork.

Being, looking, listening

Once you have all gathered at your meeting place, arrange a time when you will gather once more. A loud whistle or bell makes an effective signal to bring people together again, but a shout will do. Once the signal has been arranged, walk some distance away from each other, either alone or in small groups if accompanying young children. Ideally, within the parameters of safety, you should be far enough apart that you can no longer see or hear each other clearly.

Find a place to sit or stand comfortably, then remain as still as possible, listening to the silence. You may be able to hear sounds in the distance, or even nearby, but allow them to float past you without letting your mind focus on them or draw them into your consciousness. It is enough to recognise the noise as sound, then let your mind move on. How does it feel to be alone? Are you aware of the presence of God, or does he too seem very far from you? What would it be like to be genuinely lost? How would it feel? When you hear the signal to regather, say a short prayer for those who live in silence, whether by choice or necessity.

Collecting: twigs

Gather material to make twig stars. You will need at least five strong sticks or twigs for each star, some strands of ivy for fastening, and brightly coloured berries and moss as decorations. You may not be able to find all the materials you need, but there should be some sticks or even long stalks of grass still to be found.

CREATING: TWIG STARS

Make your twig stars by laying five sticks or twigs in the pattern of a five-pointed star, then binding the sticks together at the points of intersection—five at the outer ends of the sticks, then five more in the middle, where they cross over again. You can use strands of ivy to bind them, but it may be easier to use string.

Once your twig star bases have been firmly tied, you can decorate them with berries, moss, ivy and so on. If you prefer, you can wrap brightly coloured wool around your stars in rainbow shades. Perhaps each group of stars could be a different colour of the rainbow.

FEASTING: A FLOCK OF SHEEP

You will need:
- 45 g butter
- 300 g marshmallows
- 180 g Rice Krispies
- Black writing icing
- White mini marshmallows or black or white fondant icing
- Cupcakes (optional)
- Green buttercream icing (optional)
- Knives for spreading and moulding
- Flat dish
- Baking parchment
- Paper plates

In advance, melt the butter with the marshmallows over a low heat, before adding the Rice Krispies. Push the mixture down into a flat dish that has been generously greased with butter and the base lined with baking parchment. This is an incredibly sticky thing to do, but, as it cools, the mixture becomes less sticky and more malleable.

To make a sheep, take a handful of Rice Krispies mix and mould it into the right shape. For a more sophisticated sculpture, you can pull out some Krispies to form a head, or make a separate head then 'glue' it on with buttercream icing.

Four mini marshmallows make the feet, while one mini marshmallow cut on the diagonal will make two ears, which can be squished into place. Finish off with eyes and nose made of writing icing.

If you wish, you can extend the activity by providing a 'field' for the sheep, made from a cupcake coated with green buttercream icing.

CELEBRATING: MAKING A BUDDY BENCH

Make a 'buddy bench' for your worship space. This is an area of seating large enough for at least two people, ideally three or more. It can be made of any material, although, if it is to be a permanent feature, it needs to have some solidity. Ideally, the community should work together on the design and construction of the bench, providing raw materials and labour for the task. When it is finished, it can be decorated with the twig stars or with any of your other creations from Outdoor Church. A pergola or roof structure provides even more scope for artistic decoration and embellishment.

Once the buddy bench has been constructed, it should be put to use as soon as possible. If any member of the community feels lonely or would like a chat, they can come and sit on the buddy bench as a sign that they would like someone to talk to. One or more other members can then join together and begin a conversation. This approach has been tried very successfully with children in schools and day-care centres, but it also works well with adults in unfamiliar places. If you do not have a permanent outdoor meeting place, a buddy bench within your church building would make a wonderful place for visitors or newcomers to meet regular members of the congregation, as well as a way of enabling the church children, who may attend different schools, to meet each other.

The lost coin

'Or what woman having ten silver coins, if she loses one of them, does not light a lamp, sweep the house, and search carefully until she finds it? When she has found it, she calls together her friends and neighbours, saying, "Rejoice with me, for I have found the coin that I had lost." Just so, I tell you, there is joy in the presence of the angels of God over one sinner who repents.'

LUKE 15:8–10

Reflecting on the story

This scenario is described for us in just a few simple words, yet it has instant dramatic appeal, for it resonates with anyone who has ever lost anything even slightly valuable. As modern readers, we can substitute all sorts of things for the silver coin—car keys, passport, bank book, reading glasses or even the television remote may all spark a flurry of frantic searching, often in the most unlikely places. In the same way, Jesus says, God seeks us out, wherever we have strayed. But the parable gives us a deeper insight than simply that God looks in likely and less obvious places; it tells us more than we might first notice about the kingdom of heaven and the action of God.

The woman has only ten coins to begin with, so to lose one is to lose a tenth of her wealth. When we understand this, the lost object becomes instantly much more precious than those trivial things that first strike us as being comparable. No longer are we concerned with lost library books, but with significant treasures, upon which our future well-being depends. People are precious in God's eyes, every single one of them has infinite value for him, and he knows the instant that one has wandered away from the right path. The woman sweeps the floor to find the lost coin—a floor that may be made of beaten earth, scattered with rushes or coarsely tiled. If she had only ten silver coins, it is unlikely to be a grand mosaic pavement.

So, too, the places where we get lost may be dark and unpleasant, but God, like the woman, will not give up the search. It takes more than a grubby floor to discourage the diligent seeker. Finally, the joy when the lost object is found is great indeed; when we turn once more to God, there is rejoicing in heaven among the angels. There is no hint of punishment or even reproach, simply great celebration and relief.

Activities

Preparation

The theme of searching is continued from 'The lost sheep' in this session. Just as a silver coin might not mean a great deal to a rich person, but was a tenth of the woman's savings, so the people and things that might seem trivial to many of us are all important parts of God's creation and should be treasured as such.

Being, looking, listening

When you have arrived at your gathering place, take some time to choose where to sit or stand, then look for a natural object or group of objects that will be your focus for the session. The group can all look at one thing or individuals can select their own.

Now take time to examine the object in great detail. Look at the many different colours of the object, and the range of textures that it offers. Use all your senses to appreciate it: how does it feel and what does it smell like? Consider the great love that God has for this small piece of his universe, and how that love flows in and through the object and out into the world. If you have picked up the object, put it back where you found it and look at it in its context. How does it fit into the rest of the landscape? What does it add? Would anyone notice if it wasn't there? Would that matter?

Collecting: litter picking

Unfortunately, in almost every natural landscape there will be signs that human beings have passed that way in the unattractive and dangerous form of litter. If you are able, ask the group to come armed with protective clothing, including heavy-duty gloves, as well as dustbin sacks and, if possible, litter pickers or sharp sticks to spike debris (these can be supplied by your local council), in order to clear up the part of the environment that you are using. Spend time searching out even the smallest scrap of rubbish; it is destructive to the landscape and its inhabitants.

Creating: junk modelling

The craft continues the theme of rubbish, although it is not advisable from a safety aspect to use the litter that you have gathered from your litter pick. Ask your group to bring their recyclables from home to create a corporate junk model. It can be based on a theme—a figure, perhaps—or simply a freeform creation. Individuals can work on their own, but a group work will be bigger and will produce a good feeling of community. If you are creating the model in your outdoor space, remember to clear up all evidence of its existence once the activity is over.

Feasting: broom and coins

You will need (per cake):
- One cupcake
- Chocolate buttercream icing
- One chocolate dessert cup
- White fondant icing
- One thin biscuit stick (such as Mikado)
- One strip of flat ribbon sweet
- Rolling pin and board
- Knife for spreading
- Scissors
- Icing nozzle or very small circular cookie cutter
- Paper plate

Chocolate dessert cups can be bought from a supermarket or made by melting chocolate in a microwave (medium setting) or in a bowl over a pan of hot water, then using the chocolate to paint the insides of silicon ice-cube trays. Once set, the chocolate cups can be carefully popped out.

Both making the broom and cutting out the coins are fiddly things to do. If you have very young children, it might be better to make the alternative craft (see below).

Make ten tiny coins from the white fondant icing, using the icing nozzle to cut out circles.

Cover the cupcake with chocolate buttercream icing and smooth it as flat as possible, to make a 'floor'. Place the chocolate dessert cup on the cake and carefully put nine of the coins inside it. Put the tenth on the cake itself.

Make a broom by winding the flat sweet around one end of the biscuit stick, then carefully cutting 'bristles'. (You might find it easier to cut the bristles first.) If you dampen the end of the sweet slightly, it will stick to itself once it has been wrapped around the biscuit broomstick.

Place the broom next to the lost coin on the cake.

As an alternative craft, provide plain digestive biscuits and different colours of writing icing for the children to design their own coins. If you want to extend the craft, they can cover the digestive coin base with white fondant icing or spread it with vanilla buttercream icing first.

Celebrating: a scavenger hunt

Go on a scavenger hunt. Divide your group into as many smaller groups as you like, then give each group a list of objects to collect or photograph. The lists can be the same or different for each group. The first team to tick off every item on the list has won.

The rules are as follows:

- Don't forget that the aim of the hunt is to explore the landscape and find some of its secrets, not to be the winner at all costs.
- Groups must contain people of different ages and the group must stay and hunt for each object on the list together (although it is a good idea to let different people take it in turn to lead the hunt for each object).
- Make sure the groups know the boundaries of the hunt, in terms of both place and time.

The sort of items you look for will depend on your environment: seasides will have different objects from parkland, for example. Try to make your objects as varied as possible and include more general things, so that younger ones can sometimes take the lead in the search.

Objects to photograph could include:

- An insect
- An animal's house
- A spider's web
- Some water
- An object that is out of place

Objects to find could include:

- A seed
- Five different leaves
- Something red
- Something a bird or animal might eat
- Something with a pattern

- A feather
- Something beautiful
- Something that reminds you of a parable

Make sure that when your scavenger hunt has ended, objects are returned undamaged to their places.

The prodigal son

'There was once a man with two sons. One day, the younger son said to his father, "Let me have my share of everything I will inherit when you die. I'd like to travel and enjoy myself now." So the father divided everything that he had between his two sons.

'The younger son took his money and went far away. He used all his money enjoying himself and making lots of friends, but after a time he had spent it all.

'Then there was a terrible famine in the land. There was nothing to eat. The younger son took the only job he could find, feeding pigs. He was so hungry, he could have eaten the pigs' food. Then the young man realised how silly he was.

'"The people who work for my father have far more than I have now. I'll go home and tell him I am sorry. I will ask if I can have a job on the farm."

'But the boy's father had been watching and waiting, hoping his son would come back. He saw his son coming and ran to meet him. He threw his arms around him and hugged him.

'"I have let you down and done things I am ashamed of," the boy said. "I'm so sorry. I don't deserve to be treated as your son. Let me work for you instead."

'But his father shook his head.

'"Fetch the best clothes for my son," the father called to one of his servants. "Find new sandals and a ring for his finger. Prepare the best food! I thought my son was dead. He was lost, but now he's found. Let's have a party to celebrate his return!"'

BARNABAS CHILDREN'S BIBLE, NO. 282 (LUKE 15:11–23)

Reflecting on the story

A frequent practice in Bible study is to take a character from one of the parables and try to inhabit the mind of that character. What are they feeling and thinking, why are they acting the way they do, and in what ways am I similar to this character? This is a particularly useful exercise to practise with this parable, as each character offers insights into our own behaviour and response to God's grace. The prodigal son does not just seek the easy life of luxury; if he did, it would be simple for us to feel that we had nothing in common with him. The prodigal son does more than this. He takes what has been given to him as a gift and misuses it, just as we take our intelligence, personality and talents and behave as if they belong solely to us rather than to the one who bestowed them upon us. The older brother, who works steadily and hard while his feckless younger brother squanders all that has been given to him, resents the grace of forgiveness that is so willingly and generously extended to the younger brother when he finally returns home.

We may also be guilty of resenting the good fortune of others who seem not to have deserved such blessings, while we, who have behaved well and endured all sorts of trying circumstances, go unrecognised. When we realise that we are guilty of these things, then we may well act as the younger brother and repent, turning home to the one who has been patiently watching and waiting for us all this time. Repentance is not an occasion for reproach or remonstration, but rather a time of rejoicing. 'Repent, for the kingdom of heaven is at hand,' we are told; we are not turning away, so much as turning towards. We hear the voice of the one who loves us completely and unreservedly, calling us back home where we truly belong.

ACTIVITIES

PREPARATION

The theme of watching and waiting continues, but here the emphasis moves to looking from a distance, or for things that are a long way off. As we wait for the coming of God's kingdom, we look for signs of that coming. We gaze all around us for indications that our faith and hope are not in vain—and they are not, for even now, signs of the kingdom are present to those who see.

BEING, LOOKING, LISTENING

Find a high vantage point. This may involve climbing a tree, being careful not to damage the tree itself and climbing safely and slowly, never higher than you can easily descend from. You might go to a hilly or, better still, mountainous area. If you live in a very flat location, try to find a place where you have a clear view over the surrounding landscape. If your church building has a tower, or if there is simply a house with a very good view that you may use, these too would be good options.

When you have found your 'watchtower', look out across the landscape as far as you can see. Notice how small the trees and houses are in the distance, and how everything becomes clearer the nearer it is. Imagine what it must have been like for the father of the prodigal son as he strained his eyes day after day for a glimpse of his errant son. Picture his feelings when that first uncertain sighting became gradually clearer—a joy, says Jesus, like the joy of those in heaven when we turn towards our spiritual home, seeking God.

Collecting: bird food

Winter time is very challenging for the animals and birds that share our environment, and hunting for food becomes a full-time task for them if starvation is to be avoided. Help the birds by looking for seeds and berries that they can eat. Some birds eat small insects, too, so you could gather those if you wish. Look deep into holly bushes for the berries that the birds have missed, and pick the last few flower heads that have not fallen to the ground, taking care not to damage the plants or trees too much as you do so.

Creating: bird feeders

Make a seed cake to feed the birds, using the seeds you have gathered. Unless you have been very lucky, you will need to supplement your seeds with wild bird food, which can be purchased from supermarkets and garden centres.

Remember that wild bird seed mix will often contain nuts: check the ingredients before purchasing.

The simplest bird feeder to make uses stale wholemeal bread and honey. You can cut circle and star shapes out of slices of bread using cookie cutters. Make a hole at the edge of your bread and knot some thread through, for hanging. Spread one side of the bread with honey, then place it, honey side down, in a narrow dish filled with bird seed. Hang your seedy honey bread from a branch where you can spot the birds as they come to feed.

Alternatively, mix small pieces of chopped lard with raisins, wholemeal breadcrumbs, seeds and grated cheese, squishing everything between your fingers until it has mixed into a solid ball. The mixture can be either moulded round a piece of string or squashed into a yoghurt pot which has had a string attached to it through the base of the pot, so that it can be hung upside down. Chill in the fridge before hanging outside.

FEASTING: WATCHTOWER

You will need (per tower):
- One slice of plain cake
- One digestive biscuit
- Vanilla buttercream icing in green and grey
- Black writing icing
- One cupcake (optional)
- Knives for spreading and cutting
- Paper plate

Cut a rectangular tower shape from the cake slice. (You may want to do this in advance.) Older children may want to cut crenellations from the top; this is quite tricky and they may need to practise on more than one slice of cake before they get it just right. Once you are satisfied, carefully cover the tower with the grey buttercream icing.

Cover the digestive biscuit with green buttercream icing. Don't smooth the icing too much: it is supposed to look like grass.

Stand the tower on the green biscuit base. Using black writing icing, outline windows and a door on your tower.

If you want the tower to look as if it is on a hill, place it on top of a cupcake.

Celebrating: leaf lanterns

As the days get shorter, outdoor lighting becomes a useful accessory. Make tealight lanterns using leaves that you have collected.

Blow up a balloon, then cover it with a layer of white tissue paper, using washable PVA glue that has been thinned with water. For a second layer, arrange leaves in patterns, glueing them down before putting at least two more layers of tissue on to the balloon. When the tissue is dry, pop the balloon and cut a gap in the tissue, big enough to place a tealight inside.

Hang your lantern from a long stick, using string or thin wire, then put your tealight inside the balloon, sticking it in place with Velcro dots or Blu-tack if necessary. To avoid fire risk, battery-operated nightlights can be purchased very cheaply from large supermarkets or craft stores.

Stand the stick, with lantern attached, in the ground around your meeting space for decoration and visibility.

The house on the rock

As people listened to what Jesus had to say, the people divided into groups. Many were eager to hear more. They wanted to know how to please God. Some were suspicious or angry at this way of teaching. It was different from the teaching of the scribes and Pharisees. So Jesus told a story.

'If you listen to me and do what I say, you will be like a wise man who built his house on a rock. Before he started work, the man made sure that his house had firm foundations on the rock. Then when the rain battered against the house, and the wind blew around it, it did not collapse. It remained firm and solid.

'If you take no notice of what I have said, you will be like a foolish man who built his house on sand. When the wind blew and the rain beat against his house, it had no foundations and so it fell down. The walls and roof, the door and all his belongings were swept away.

'Don't be like the foolish man, regretting his mistake when it is too late to change things. Be like the wise man; listen well and act on what you hear.'

BARNABAS CHILDREN'S BIBLE, NO. 265 (LUKE 6:46–49)

Reflecting on the story

Our local school, oversubscribed due to its excellent reputation, needed to expand. Detailed plans were drawn up and explained to parents, staff and pupils; budgets were carefully assigned. Finally the great day came when the construction began—except that it didn't, because, as far as the perplexed pupils could see, nothing was being built at all. Rather, the opposite was happening, as the builders dug deeper and deeper into the ground. It was only after some considerable time that finally the bricklayers arrived, to the delight of all who had watched the building's progress. The walls went up rapidly compared with the time spent below ground level, and there was a grand opening when the extension was finally complete.

That's the problem with foundations: they are a great deal of hard work, take much time and effort to build, and there seems to be nothing much to show for them. It sometimes seems like that with our prayer life too. We spend time in church, studying the Bible, patiently praying, and, to all intents and purposes, nothing much happens. But firm foundations are not needed for sunny days, when things are going well and life seems pleasant and easy. The very flimsiest of shelters will do then, just as the very shallowest of beliefs will be sufficient. It is easy to slip into a sort of transactional relationship with God almost without being aware of it: 'I will pray for this and this and this, and because I go to church regularly, and study, and give to charity, I will surely get what I have asked for.'

When the storms break over our heads, when the waters rise, and when our happiness, our security and even our lives are in danger, however, then is the time when the hours of prayer and study are shown to have taken root in our souls. Just as a structure with its foundations deep in the ground can withstand tempests, so can we find the strength to continue, relying on God's strength when ours fails, believing always in his presence, even when it is not obvious.

Activities

Preparation

During the coldest time of year, it may seem a lot of trouble to venture outside, putting on layers of clothing before trudging through a frozen landscape for a brief time before the temperature dips too far and we must return home. However short the expedition, though, the changing landscape will present its own marvels, and the strength of the rocks and of the water frozen into ice leads us once more into wonder.

Being, looking, listening

The miracle of water gradually becoming more and more solid until it forms a block of ice is so familiar to us that there is a danger we will take it for granted. When the weather is appropriately cold, go on an ice hunt. Look for puddles of water that have frozen over, trapping air bubbles beneath. If the puddle is shallow and boots are being worn, tread on the ice slowly and gently, focusing on the sensation of a slippery surface, followed by a gradual cracking as the ice shivers and breaks. Rivers and ponds, although they may not freeze completely, may leave deposits of ice at the edges. Look for streams of water with frozen surfaces but still running beneath, and notice how the water surges and flows beneath the ice. See if you can spy icicles hanging from branches or shrubs; warm them in your hands and watch them slowly melt and begin to drip.

Remember that the safety rules for water apply even more strictly in the case of frozen streams and rivers. Ice is rarely thick enough in this country to support the weight of a human being, and you should never walk on a frozen surface unless you are sure that the water beneath it is only a few inches deep, such as you find in puddles.

If you do not have access to natural ice, bags of ice cubes can be purchased quite cheaply, and bowls of ice can be explored. See what happens when salt is added, or when trickles of warm water are poured on to an ice cube.

Collecting: stones

Look for stones that have attractive and interesting shapes. Ideally the stones you collect should have one surface that is relatively flat, so that they will balance easily. Find ones that look like animals, perhaps with protuberances like noses or hollows where eyes might go. The larger they are, the easier the craft will be, but take care not to alter or damage the landscape by removing too many. This is particularly important if you are hunting along pebble or rocky beaches: too much of our seaside landscape is being eroded by people seeking garden decorations.

Creating: stone creatures

Make a stone animal or person. You can use natural materials such as wood and moss for limbs and fur, or provide a supply of craft materials such as googly eyes, feathers, pompoms, wool and pipe cleaners. Acrylic paint gives the best coverage for stones, although poster paints can give a colourwash effect and have the advantage of washing off clothes as well.

Do not try to make the animals accurate renditions of real creatures. Let your imagination run wild, using the natural shapes and colours of the stones themselves as a springboard for your creativity.

Feasting: Battenberg house

Warning: this cake is not suitable for nut allergy sufferers.

You will need (per house):
- One mini Battenberg cake
- 1 dsp vanilla buttercream icing
- Sweets to decorate
- One digestive biscuit
- 1 dsp green buttercream icing
- Blue writing icing
- Knives for spreading and cutting
- Paper plate

Younger children may need the Battenbergs to be cut to shape before they start.

Cut the mini Battenberg in half across its width, then cut one of the halves across the diagonal, to form a triangular roof shape. Check that the roof and the second Battenberg half, which will form the main part of the house, go together neatly, trimming them carefully if necessary.

On the house walls, make windows and doors, using writing icing, jelly sweets cut to shape or other decorations. You can add more sweets as borders or embellishments for the house.

Once you have finished decorating the walls, place the roof on top. When you are happy with the way they look, attach the roof to the house walls using the vanilla buttercream.

Spread the digestive biscuit with green buttercream, patting it gently to get a rough grass-like effect. Carefully place the house on top of the biscuit.

If you feel ambitious, you can pipe blue 'waves' of writing icing around the edges of the digestive biscuit.

Celebrating: building a cairn

One of the most famous Christian pilgrimage routes in the world is the road to the Spanish city of Santiago de Compostela. Hundreds of thousands of people travel along this route each year, and many of them add to the piles of stones or rocks that form cairns along the journey. They might do this to mark a stage on their journey, as a visible sign that they were there, or as a symbol of a prayer offered or answered.

Encourage each member of the group to find a stone from the area and to examine it carefully. If you wish, the stones can be painted, but, if they are going to remain outside, it is probably better for them to remain undecorated. Place the stones in a heap as a sign that the group was present, as a marker of faith and as a sign of commitment to their spiritual journey.

Winter celebration: Candlemas

When Jesus was just over a month old, Mary and Joseph prepared to take him to the temple in Jerusalem. They went to thank God for his safe birth and offer a sacrifice of two pigeons.

As they went into the temple courts, they met there a man called Simeon. Simeon had been waiting for the day when God would send his Messiah—the chosen one who would save his people. He believed that God had promised him that he would see this Saviour before he died.

When Simeon saw Mary and Joseph and the baby boy in their arms, he knew that the special day had arrived. He took Jesus from them and praised God.

'Lord, you can let me now die in peace, because I have seen with my own eyes the Saviour you have promised your people. This child will reveal your truth to all people on earth and be everything the Jewish nation have been waiting for.'

Mary and Joseph listened in some surprise to his words but before they had taken it all in, an elderly woman approached them. Anna was a prophetess who had lived in the temple, praying and worshipping God for most of her long life. She also knew that Jesus was God's chosen one. And she thanked God for him.

Mary and Joseph made their offering. They wondered at all they had learned that day about their baby son.

BARNABAS CHILDREN'S BIBLE, NO. 249 (LUKE 2:22–40)

Reflecting on the story

The feast of Candlemas falls at the most depressing time of the year. Christmas is finished and Lent lies over the horizon; seasonal bills are coming in, the days are still short and signs of hope seem few and far between. Yet into this breaks the festival of light, celebrating the recognition among people of the old covenant that the new covenant has arrived, and, with it, the hope of the entire world. Mary and Joseph's dutiful expedition to the temple brings a reward for years of patient waiting for Simeon and Anna, who see, in the most unlikely child of ordinary parents, the salvation of the nations.

Candlemas falls halfway between the winter solstice and the spring equinox and is looked on by many as the beginning of spring. With its promise of longer days and new growth, it is a sign that God has kept his promise of sending a Messiah, a light into the darkness and sorrow of the world.

Traditionally the stock of candles for the church was blessed at this festival, and candles are still lit for the procession towards the font, which reminds us of our hope in Christ, the gift of redemption shared freely with us, and that we too have a part to play in bringing the kingdom of God closer. 'Shine like a light in the world,' we are told at our baptism, and it is our role to show, by our actions and words, by our community of prayer and thanksgiving, that the love of Christ brings hope for all.

Yet this sign of hope brings with it a warning: Simeon tells Mary that a sword will pierce her own soul (Luke 2:35). At the end of the Candlemas celebration, we extinguish our candles as we look towards Lent, Good Friday and the challenge of the cross. Candlemas is not just a festival for one day, but a reminder that we must live different kinds of lives, knowing the danger that took Christ to the cross but secure in the love that led him there.

This session can also be used to celebrate St Lucy's Day on 13 December, which was considered the winter solstice before calendar reform. A festival observed particularly in Scandinavia, the theme for this feast is also that of light, as a girl wearing a white dress and red sash, with a wreath of candles on her head, leads a candlelit procession.

Activities

Preparation

The UK gets an average of 33 days of snowfall per year, with most of it falling on higher ground. Cornwall gets the fewest days, at just ten. Over the whole of England there are only about 16 days when snow actually lies on the ground, although this figure rises to 27 in Scotland. The rarity of white-covered ground makes it imperative that snowfalls are celebrated—if not at Candlemas itself, then by holding a festival of snow and light whenever the opportunity presents itself.

Being, looking, listening

Go out into the snow and explore it. Open your mouth and try to catch a snowflake on your tongue, feeling its icy cold before your warmth melts it. Make snow angels by lying in the snow and moving your arms up and down and your legs from side to side. Make a company of snow angels and decorate them with fir cones, ivy stems, acorns and pebbles. Have a snowball fight, taking care not to hit people in the face, or aim snowballs at tree trunks, or try to knock down columns of snow with snowballs if a fight seems to be inviting trouble. Build snowmen, small or large, and give them features with personality. Climb to the top of a slope and slide down it—on a tray or dustbin sack if you don't have a sledge.

If there is plenty of snow, try making a snow house; if there is not very much snow, make a snow den for an animal or a toy.

Find a clear patch of snow and make patterns with your feet and hands, then find other objects that will make patterns in the snow. Play giant snow noughts and crosses with sticks and stones, or make a long-jump pitch. Draw pictures in the snow, using spray bottles filled with warm water to make melted lines, or adding food colouring to make coloured shapes.

Collecting: decorative objects

Collect objects to put in an ice candleholder. They will need to be quite small so that they fit into the mould, but they can include berries, sticks, leaves or tiny feathers—anything that looks attractive.

CREATING: ICE CANDLEHOLDER

To make an ice candleholder, you will need two containers, one slightly larger than the other. Glass beakers are best, with a small shot glass fitting comfortably into a tumbler. If you plan to use battery-operated candles, make sure the small glass is big enough to hold one comfortably.

Place the smaller glass into the larger one, ensuring that it fits properly. Carefully pour water into the gap between the glasses until the rim of the small glass is level with the rim of the larger one. Fix the small glass in place with strong tape. You may need to weight the smaller glass with beads or small stones to stop it floating too high.

Carefully insert your collected objects in the gap between the two glasses, trying to use a mixture of objects that will sink to the bottom, such as berries, and objects that will float in the sides, such as leaves and twigs. Freeze the glasses, ideally in a patch of snow outside, but in your freezer if this isn't possible.

To extract your candleholder, pour hot (not boiling) water into the small glass first, gently loosening it before removing it. Then pour hot water round the outside of the large glass so that the ice melts just enough for you to remove the glass.

FEASTING: A ST LUCY WREATH

You will need (per wreath):
- One ring doughnut (mini ones are preferable for smaller children)

- White chocolate fingers or candy sticks (in proportion to the size of doughnut)
- Strawberry leather and vanilla candy melts, white chocolate or buttercream (optional, to make 'flames')
- Writing icing, jelly sweets, fondant icing and so on
- Scissors or knife for cutting strawberry leather
- Paper plate

If you decide to make strawberry leather 'flames', you might want to cut these out beforehand.

Make a St Lucy wreath by sticking white chocolate finger 'candles' into a ring doughnut, which can then be decorated with writing icing, jelly sweets, fondant icing leaves and so on. If you wish, you can add strawberry leather 'flames' to the top of the biscuit, attaching them with a dab of buttercream or, better still, melted white chocolate or vanilla candy melts.

Celebrating: a night hike

Go on a night hike. You may have to scout out the route first, depending on the age and mobility of your group. It is best to begin with a level path that is as even as possible—perhaps through a park or meadow or along a well-worn track. Later, as you become more experienced, more adventurous terrain can be explored.

Be sure to count the members of your group and to have a designated front and back marker, ideally in reflective jackets. The aim is to undertake the walk using only the natural light of moon and stars, so a clear night would be helpful. Group members may bring torches, and certainly the leader and markers should have large, bright torches, but these should not be turned on except in an emergency or the group's night vision will be affected.

Walk slowly and carefully, pausing frequently to listen to the sounds of the night—nightjars and owls, for example, or the rustle of small animals disturbed by your progress. You may be aware of bats or owls flying low above your heads, or birds roosting in the trees. Look up at the stars and try to identify the major ones—the North Star, certainly. If you are walking near the sea, listen for the sound of the waves against the shore, and try to walk a few steps in rhythm with the sea itself.

If you are walking to your gathering place, arrange to have it lit with candles and torches, perhaps even a campfire, so that the group can approach the light from the darkness of the surrounding landscape.

Prayer suggestions

Create a prayer space

The whole of an Outdoor Church event is an action prayer, and there should be no concern if a space for formal, spoken prayers cannot be found within the structure of an event. However, you may find it helpful to provide opportunities for quiet reflection, either individually or corporately.

Perhaps you could create a prayer space within the Outdoor Church worship area. This could be a place that is slightly set apart from the main areas of activity, although, for reasons of safety, it should not be entirely cut off from the action or completely enclosed. It might be partly roofed, and you might want to indicate the boundaries of the area with willow fencing or posts. You could create a fence with string or ivy stems, and hang leaves or decorative objects from it. Within the space, you might want to place some objects that can encourage reflection—a basket of stones, for example, or a flowering plant. If possible, plant a variety of flowers that will bloom in each season, providing a constantly changing focal point.

Participants in an Outdoor Church event can be encouraged to take time out within the prayer space, reflecting on their experiences or simply taking the opportunity to be quiet in creation.

Prayer activities

There are many useful resources available for interactive prayers, including those specifically for outdoor use. BRF's Messy Church books offer many creative ideas and suggestions, and there are also specific books on creative prayer, such as *80 Creative Prayer Ideas* by Claire Daniel (BRF, 2014).

Here are a few prayer activities that might be particularly suitable for specific Outdoor Church occasions.

Landscape prayers

God of wilderness and pastures, fields and woodlands, hear our prayer.

Spread out as many pictures of different landscapes as you can find. They can be cut from magazines and newspapers, or you can simply provide books open at pages with different kinds of scenery depicted on them.

Place the pictures of different landscapes where the group can see them. Ask people to spend five minutes in silence just looking at the huge variety.

Invite individuals to select just one picture and hold it in their hands. Ask them to think about the landscape, the people who might live in it and the joys and challenges that inhabiting such a place might bring.

If they wish, people can write down some thoughts or reflections on sticky notes and put them on the pictures.

For signs and for seasons and for days and years (Genesis 1:14).

As the group members walk to the Outdoor Church space, ask them to collect signs of new growth. This should be done sensitively and sparingly, so that minimum damage is done to the plants. Alternatively, photographs can be taken so that even less damage is caused.

On arriving at the worship space, invite each member to bring their offering and place it on the altar or in the central worship space, together with their landscape pictures and reflections (if they wrote any). You can make the pile as untidy or as attractive as you want, mixing up the pictures with the objects or keeping them separate.

God of landscapes, we thank you for the infinite variety of your creation. Let us always respond to it with thankfulness and awareness of the blessings that you pour upon us, even when the challenges of living in certain places seem harsh or uncomfortable. We offer these signs of new growth and life to you, and ask that you bless those who work on the land to produce food and crops for the benefit of all humankind. We pray for spiritual growth and ask that you bless this community as we look together at the wonderful things you have made. Amen

CARING FOR CREATION

Prepare the area by placing bowls of soil, water, seeds and fruit (such as grapes or berries) in the space. Arrange the bowls carefully so that they provide an attractive focal point for prayer. As each prayer is offered, ask a member of the group to hold the relevant bowl. If you have a small group, you could invite people to put their hands into each bowl and feel the contents.

Seeds

Lord of all created things, we pray for all creatures who are at the beginning of life and those who take care of them. We thank you for the ability to grow and change, and we ask your blessing on us as we seek to become more like you.

Soil

Help us to remember that you are with us even in the dark times. Help us to believe in the light, even when we cannot see it. Give us patience and faith in your love.

Water

Thank you for the things that make us grow in faith—for the words of wisdom we read and hear, for the experience of others, and the knowledge of your Holy Spirit surrounding us in love.

Fruit

We celebrate the fruitfulness of your creation, Lord, and we bring our gifts and talents to your service. We pray that we may use all that we have been given to the glory of your kingdom.

Prayer trails

Make a prayer trail around your church or your outside worship area. Beginning at the entrance to the space, travel to three or four different points, ending at the altar or focal point of the worship space.

Beginning

Give each participant a candle, either a wax one or a small electric nightlight. Ask them to light their candles as a sign that they actively seek the light of God's love and wish to learn to live by it. Take the lighted candles on the journey with you.

'Arise, shine; for your light has come, and the glory of the Lord has risen upon you' (Isaiah 60:1). Guide us as we seek your kingdom, Lord. Help us to journey in the light of your love, so that we can see the path that lies before us.

Pause for prayer (1)

Turn off or extinguish the candles. Ask the participants to reflect on those times when they have not sought God's kingdom.

We are sorry, Lord, for those times when our hearts have not sought your treasure, but have longed for other things. We regret our greed, our selfishness and our refusal to share the gifts that you have given us. Forgive us, Father, and lead us to the true treasure.

Relight the candles before moving on to the next stopping point.

Pause for prayer (2)

Give your candle to another person in the group, receiving in turn a candle from someone else.

Help us to share the good news of your kingdom with those we meet. Let us not seek to keep your treasure to ourselves, but to rejoice that all may share in your eternal love.

Arriving

Place the lit candles on or around the altar or worship area.

Father God, you journey with us as we search for the treasure of your kingdom, and you share our joy when we find it. Keep us faithful to our quest, trusting in your loving companionship.

Seedtime and harvest

Gather as many different seeds as possible, ideally with pictures of what they will look like when fully grown. Seed packets are very useful for this, and many people will be only too pleased to donate packets of out-of-date seeds from their garden shed. If you can, download some images of seeds viewed under a microscope (some can be found in Wikimedia Commons, a copyright-free website). If you can, get a bowlful of one type of seed, such as popcorn or sunflower seeds, which can be bought at supermarkets.

Invite participants to run their fingers through the seeds in the large bowl. How do they feel? What do they look like?

Creator God, there are so many millions of seeds on this planet, all containing the potential to be plants. So too do we contain potential. Help us to live our lives in ways that encourage this potential, and to realise it through your love.

Now examine an individual seed. See how small it is when compared to the plant it will become.

God of tiny things, help us to notice the small signs of your kingdom here on earth. May we appreciate acts of kindness and generosity and carry them out ourselves, so that your kingdom grows ever greater.

Look at a picture of a seed under a microscope. Notice how brightly coloured they are and what wonderful shapes they have.

So many seeds, Lord, and all different, but evidence of your care can be seen even in these tiny creations, as yet unfulfilled. Help us to remember that your love for each one of us is unique, and that your tender care will nourish and sustain us as we grow towards your light.

Feather prayers

'Look at the birds of the air' (Matthew 6:26).

Gather together a collection of feathers, as many different types as possible. Either share them among the group or display them where they can easily be seen by everyone. Alternatively, if you have access to an overhead projector, you might show suitable examples.

Notice how different the feathers are from each other; that is because they have different purposes. Find a feather that might be used as a way of showing off to attract a mate. It might be a feather that is brightly coloured, like a peacock's tail, or red, like a robin's breast. Everyone wants to be popular, and we enjoy being friends with people. Sometimes, however, our desire to be friends can make us behave in ways that are not so good.

Lord God, we thank you for the friends we have, and the company of others. Help us not to be so proud of ourselves that we ignore the gifts of others, nor to try so hard to make new friends that we take no notice of the ones we have.

Some feathers are designed to camouflage the bird. They may be speckled, like the light shining through tree branches, or a dull brown, like tree trunks. Sometimes we don't want to be noticed. We might be feeling shy, or nervous of a new situation.

Courageous God, help us to be aware of your presence with us when we find ourselves in new or difficult situations. Give us courage in our encounters and an openness to what they might bring.

Find a small feather with a downy end. Feel how soft it is and how warm. These feathers protect a bird from the cold and provide a soft cover for eggs and baby birds.

Father God, we thank you for your protecting love. Help us to feel that we are held safe by you at all times.

I call on you, my God, for you will answer me;
turn your ear to me and hear my prayer.
Show me the wonders of your great love,
you who save by your right hand
those who take refuge in you from their foes.
Keep me as the apple of your eye;
hide me in the shadow of your wings.

PSALM 17:6–8 (NIV)

ALSO BY SALLY WELCH

Celebrating Festivals

ISBN 9781841017112

£8.99

ALSO BY SALLY WELCH

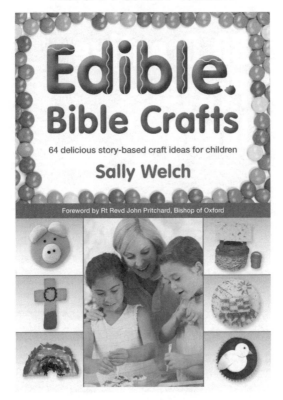

Edible Bible Crafts

ISBN 9780857462435

£11.99

ALSO FROM BRF

80 Creative Prayer Ideas

ISBN 9781841016887

£8.99

Also from BRF

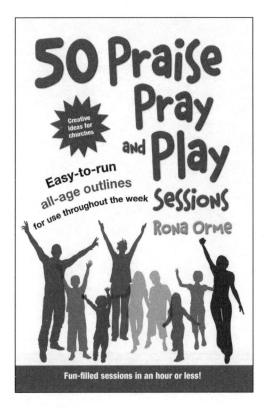

50 Praise, Pray and Play Sessions

ISBN 9781841016627

£9.99

ALSO FROM BRF

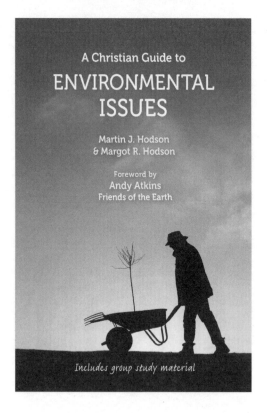

A Christian Guide to Environmental Issues

ISBN 9780857463838

£9.99